TARTS WITH TOPS ON
OR HOW TO MAKE THE PERFECT PIE

For Rob
I would rather have a crust and a tent with you
than be Queen of all the world.

Isabel Arundell to Sir Richard Burton

Eaten I have; and though I had good cheer,
I did not sup, because no friends were there.
Where mirth and friends are absent when we dine
Or sup, there wants the incense and the wine.

Robert Herrick, *Meat Without Mirth*

TARTS WITH TOPS ON
OR HOW TO MAKE THE PERFECT PIE

Tamasin Day-Lewis

Photography by David Loftus

WEIDENFELD & NICOLSON

Pies are the business. You can dress them up or dress them down. Make them classic or modern, savoury or sweet, shroud them in butter-crisp pastry or top them with creamy potato. No food comforts and nurtures like a proper homemade pie.

Tamasin Day-Lewis

Contents

Introduction 6

After I had put the tart to bed, following a year of wanton and somewhat shameful abandon, I decided enough was enough. It was time to move on, find a different muse, not subject those around me to any further helpings of this most voluptuous but repetitive form, irresistible though it be. *The Art of the Tart*, untoppable title aside, was a heavenly consummation of all things containable within the buttery, crisp crust of a pastry shell. Wobbling, unctuous, the egg yolk and ivory cream liaison setting to a breath away from liquidity, holding all inside it in suspension, deliquescent as it meets the palate, the tart is as sensuous a food as its name suggests, but, acres of pastry later, my relationship with the tart – and pastry – had come to an end.

Two books have superseded it, *Simply the Best*, a selection of articles and recipes from my weekly column in the *Daily Telegraph*, and *Good Tempered Food*, a book reaffirming the pleasures of the kitchen; of the long, slow, satisfying processes that, with the right ingredients, make for the greatest of culinary experiences; a reveille for a return to the bedrock of kitchen skills, marinading, macerating, braising, stewing, waiting, preparing a little now, a little later; for tomorrow, the next day, a feast in a few days time. I had begun to feel that the words 'quick', 'fast', 'easy', 'simple' had hijacked the culinary lexicon, and no one seemed willing to give people permission to get into the kitchen and actually enjoy the process of cooking. Cooking had become something you did while you waited for real life to happen, whereas to people like me its whole pleasure and purpose is an end in itself. But where to go next? And what could have induced me to take on a subject which historically, and on superficial acquaintance, is really about encasing, shrouding, covering and protecting fish, fowl, meat, game, vegetables, fruit or cheese under a mantle of pastry?

A 'coffyn' of pastry, a suet pudding, a pot pie, a priddy oggy, a pasty, a torta, a raised pie, a glazed pie, a potato or filo crust, the generic word 'pie' covers more than mere flour and butter would suggest. But I have to admit to being thoroughly unconvinced when first asked to consider the possibility. Eric Treuille and Rosie Kindersley at my favourite cookery book shop, Books for Cooks in Notting Hill, mentioned that the book they were most often asked for but didn't have was a definitive book of pies. I recoiled at the whole 'Olde Englishe Pyeishness' of it all, at the idea of translating phoney heritage culture into something current and of its time. At the unrelenting heaviness-of-being of the dish, and of its creator after testing it in all its manifestations: lard, butter, more lard, oil, suet, lard; you get the picture. I placed the idea swiftly and firmly on my mental back burner and decided the whole notion of a pie book was – apart from the déjà vu

Introduction

element, the lurking suspicion that this was really a second bite of the cherry, a tarts-with-tops-on riff – just not a boulevard I felt like rolling up.

One day, when I was back browsing in Books for Cooks, Eric and Rosie started getting at me again, with the disarmingly gentle technique that spelled terrier underneath. You know the sort of thing: 'you will do this book or else'; 'the customers are begging for it', 'we'll sell thousands, after all, the tart was a classic, and so could this one be'. Rosie showed me a few disparate snippets to fire the imagination, suggested several good reference books on the subject, reminded me of the fact that things like Shepherd's Pie, Cottage Pie, Fish Pie are, in fact, the veritable arteries of our culinary life. I began to think: when is a pie not a pie? And I began to realize that it didn't end with the pastry. Anything secreted under a crust could apply for membership, potato being an obvious honorary fellow, but there are also the single crust rather than double crust tarts-with-tops-on kind of pies to consider, Black Bottom Pie springing immediately to mind. And how can one equate the tender leaves of a filo parcel, with a mouthful of melting blue cheese and leeks, with a classic Apple Pie or a Beefsteak and Oyster Pudding?

There should be nothing retro or self-consciously recherché about this truly traditional form of cooking – like roasting, one of the few culinary methodologies that the British actually excel at. And there is really no excuse for us not having perfected it, given the quality of the best of our killer-filler ingredients: our beef, pork and mutton; our wild fowl and game; our seawater and freshwater fish; our soft fruits and firm fruits; our cheeses. Then there's our climate, a serious appetite stimulant if ever there was one to this most noble form of kitchen arts.

What could be more tempting than a classic Steak and Kidney Pie, the meat trapped in its sea of wine-dark gravy, a faint, yet full-on scent of kidney, a lingering bouquet? A soothing Chicken Pie, the ivory flesh gently poached, with a back note of celery, leek, onion and carrot, a velvet mantle of béchamel, enriched with cream and the poaching liquor. A turret of raised hot water crust pie, all crisp crumbliness without and soft yielding whiteness within, where sharp apples bite the richness of moist pork, musky sage and sharp, dry cider. Perfect picnic or wild walk fodder. The sugar-topped exuberance of a fruit pie, its crackling sweetness concealing the acid fruit below – green gooseberry or rhubarb, or perhaps a plate pie of morello cherries, their juices bleeding into the cornflour, comingling into a river of gummy-sweet thickness. Or the buttery spiced whiff of an Apple Pie, cloves, nutmeg and cinnamon, warming orange and lemon zest, a scoop of clotted cream about to slip and slide from its summit into a puddle below. A more minimalist parcel of filo pastry that breaks like a shower of glass in the mouth, trailing lactic-sharp goat's cheese and buttery green spinach in its wake.

One thing was for sure, if I decided to go ahead, the reality would mean baking enough pies over the ensuing months to test the resistance of the most obsessive and devoted of pie munchers.

I began, as one so often does, with culinary memories, with childhood, reminding myself of some of the pies that I have loved the longest. I re-conjured the comfort zone they wrap around one, be it winter or summer, savoury or sweet. My great friend Anne remembers that she didn't really feel she'd grown up until she was offered cream with her fruit pies. As a child, custard went up to the nursery, cream stayed downstairs in the dining room. She is someone whose early deprivations have clearly left an indelible mark. To this day she pours a lake of cream on her puddings, in the way of someone who believes they could be embarking upon their last supper.

My earliest pie memory is of running down the road to 'Joan's dad', the baker, and of being allowed down the corridor that ran between the shop and the bakery and into the floury, steamy heat of this warm hub of yeasted things. There I watched him wielding a long paddle with all the grace of a pole vaulter as he flicked a tray of buns, doughnuts or loaves in or out of the huge brick- fired oven. My real treat was his hot meat pie, a sheath of golden puff pastry that adhered instantly to the roof of the mouth, scorching, burning, clinging, the pain turning my eyes to blear – the indecent haste with which I always ate his pies never diminished over the years – and inside, a bubbling brown pond of gravy, mince and onion. Simple, basic, unrefined; food to offer ballast, succour, plenitude. Which was a problem, because I always had to go home with my errand, the bread, and eat lunch as though nothing had happened, as though I hadn't just consumed two zillion calories of high-kilowatt carbo-substance, but was starving and raring to eat the same amount all over again.

Then there were the Shepherd's and Cottage Pies, their browned, ploughed-field tops crunchy and buttery; Fish Pies with that classic ingredient of its time, anchovy sauce, shaken pinkly, sludgily from a bottle. My brother Daniel used to secrete his fish pie in pockets, handkerchiefs, my plate, anywhere. I did the same with corn beef hash, the nadir of my childhood meals.

But flapping a blanket of white pastry over a bed of thick-cut apples, the rucked surface of the apples making waves of the pastry above, an 'A' and a leafed apple cut jaggedly from the leftover overhang of pastry, was an entirely fulfilling activity, and one which doubtless influenced my love of food and cooking in no small way. Cutting, shaping, pasting and sticking are essential basic skills, invaluable to one's kitchen career, coaxing one to cook and love food, play with it, learn about it, have fun with it. As is the foreplay in the garden, a thing denied to most people, but an essential if you, like me, love to nurture the food from conception to fruition on the plate as tenderly and comprehensively as you can. Picking the soft, voluptuous summer fruits from my grandparents' canes was as much a part of kitchen lore as the cooking itself. I remember best the scent of the currants picked warm from the branch, splurting purple juices on fingers and mouths, then stripping the sun-ripened orbs from the stem with a fork, rolling them in the gritty sugar that would breathe its sweetness into their acidity just so, turning the sharpness into a mere undercurrent.

The feel of food is often overlooked, but I see it as of crucial importance to the cook at all stages, particularly in the face of so much gadgetry that, should we want to, we could replace all physical processes, cook without ever touching the food at all. Well, I have to confess, but not out of any sense of misplaced martyrdom, that the more I cook, the more I touch. I stab, I prod, I stroke, I turn, I feel, I squeeze, I massage. And the more I touch, the less I use the panoply of gadgets sitting in my kitchen. Flour and butter between the fingers, just the tips working the cold butter until you sloosh on water and, one handed, scoop and mould the soft, pliable pastry until it just coheres – that is something I've come back to, to enjoy. And it's as quick as switching on a machine that can't create the texture that your fingers can anyway, and then you have to wash it up with all its bits. Of course I get the tools out sometimes, particularly when I'm feeding the five thousand, but handmade is a cut above.

Enough. Get to it. Even if you think life's too short to stuff a mushroom, don't believe it's too short to make a pie. Cheat if you have to, though pastry made without butter, when butter it should be, is not even an apology for the real thing. Don't believe it'll take too long, that you can't make pastry, or any of those other excuses that people offer by way of justification. There are occasions when only a pie will do, and only a homemade pie at that. The way to his heart? The way to everyone's heart, and for once the seasons are levellers rather than indicators. Plum pie in the early autumn, the fruit in its after-the-fall state of collapse, intense, subtly spiced, flooded with juice; mutton and caper pudding, the mid-winter magic of an earlier era made contemporary; a spring vegetable parcel of herbs, crumbled goat's cheese and soft, scorched piquillo peppers; a summer torta, turned out warm from its tin, all buttery filo, tender young vegetables, rice, olive oil, Parmigiano and sharp-scented lemon zest. Take the line of least resistance. It's utterly irresistible.

Tamasin Day-Lewis

Is there anyone who doesn't inwardly melt at the sight of a golden glazed pie crust, with its little cottage chimney of steam wafting the scent of buried juices, the auguries of delight of what lies beneath? There is something so recondite about making a pie, and yet its image is dainty-dish, nursery-rhyme redolent of comfort and simplicity, 'as American as apple pie', 'as easy as pie'. The image of the pie is somehow quaint, romantic, one we feel nostalgic for; it is old-fashioned, welcoming, the cosiness we imagine when we are homesick, lovesick. The prinking and crimping and rolling and baking, the making and shaping by hand, the crafting of the crust are all about feeling, smelling, touching and tapping.

SAVOURY PIES

When looking for a seminal dish to begin this book and so define it – a classic, a comforter, a familiar – there was a field of one: the chicken pie. With its crisp lardy pastry shrouding the silky, ivory depths of gently poached chicken and cream, jewels of soft blanched vegetables, a whiff of aniseedy tarragon spiking the béchamel, all contrasting taste, texture, hidden colour, this is the ultimate savoury pie, unimprovable, unimpeachable, and just unbelievably good. The beginning, the end, the mother of all pies.

Chicken Pie

SERVES 4

1.5kg/3¼lb organic free-range chicken and some extra carrots, celery, onions and herbs
2 medium carrots, sliced into thick discs
2 stalks celery, chopped
2 fat white wands of leeks, sliced into discs (use tops when poaching chicken)
2 medium onions, peeled and quartered
55g/2oz unsalted butter
55g/2oz flour
150ml/5fl oz full-cream milk
150ml/5fl oz chicken stock from poaching the bird, reduced by half by boiling
150ml/5fl oz double cream
sprigs of tarragon and flat-leaf parsley, chopped
sea salt and black pepper
shortcrust pastry made with 340g/12oz plain flour and either 170g/6oz unsalted butter or lard, or half butter and half lard (see p.140)
beaten egg for glaze

Put the chicken in a tightish-fitting pot with some leek tops, carrot, celery, onion, a few peppercorns and a bouquet of fresh herbs. Just cover with water, bring to the boil slowly and skim. Cover the pan and poach the chicken for 45–60 minutes, turning it over at half time. Make the pastry, working it quickly into a ball, then wrap it in clingfilm and put it in the fridge for half an hour.

Steam the vegetables by throwing them into the steamer in the order in which they cook, carrots first, celery next, then the onion and leek for the last 5 minutes. Preheat the oven to 180°C/350°F/ Gas 4 and place a baking sheet on the middle shelf of the oven to heat up.

When the bird has cooled down sufficiently to handle, remove all the flesh you can from the bones, peeling off the skin as you go to use with the carcass to make more intensely flavoured stock the second time around. Tear the flesh along the grain, almost pulling it into long bite-sized pieces.

Make a roux with the butter and flour, then add the milk and chicken stock, both hot, alternately, until you have a satin-thick sauce. Stirring as you go, cook the sauce long enough to get rid of the flouriness, then stir in the cream. Remove from the heat, season and add the chopped fresh herbs, a couple of tablespoons of each. Stir in the chicken and vegetables and leave to cool.

Line your buttered pastry tin or pie dish with two-thirds of the rolled-out pastry, then scrape in the filling and spread it out evenly over the pastry base. Cover with the remaining third of the pastry, and crimp the edges together with the tines of a fork dipped in cold water. Brush the top with beaten egg. Cut a cross in the middle of the pie right through the pastry to allow the steam to escape as the pie

cooks. If your pie is deep rather than shallow, a china bird placed in the middle of the pie under the slashes is a good idea.

Bake for about an hour, then check. If the pastry is beautifully bronzed, cover the top with a sheet of greaseproof paper and cook for about another 15 minutes, or until your nose tells you that it is ready. Pastry does smell ready when it is! Don't cut into the pie for at least 10 minutes after taking it out of the oven.

Simpler than the classic chicken pie, and with a single upper
crust, you can make this pie with tongue or, as is preferred
nowadays, cooked ham. It has a gentle, mild simplicity. The
unthickened chicken stock is the only lubricant, making it
a cream-free, unenriched cousin to the original.

Welsh Chicken and Leek Pie

SERVES 6

1 organic chicken

110g/4oz cooked sliced tongue
or ham

1 onion, peel on

2 tbsp celery, strung
and chopped

a bouquet of fresh herbs,
parsley, thyme, bay and
rosemary

the whites of 6 leeks, well
cleaned

2 tbsp flat-leaf parsley, finely
chopped

sea salt and black pepper

shortcrust pastry made with
170g/6oz flour and 85g/3oz
unsalted butter, or half
butter and half lard (see
p.140)

beaten egg for glaze

Put the whole chicken, breast down, into a large pot, with the onion,
celery, bouquet of herbs and seasoning. Add just enough water to
cover and simmer on top of the stove until the chicken is cooked.
Let everything in the pot cool down. Take the chicken out and skin
it. Remove the legs, breasts and thighs and pull the flesh into pieces
along the grain of the meat. Skim the fat from the stock. Cut the
tongue or ham into chunky pieces.

Preheat the oven to 220°C/425°F/Gas 7. Cut the leeks into short
lengths and steam until tender. Add them, with the ham or tongue,
to the chicken in the pie dish and scatter over the parsley. Season and
pour over some stock just to reach the top of the filling.

Roll out the pastry, then cut a strip and place it around the rim
of the pie dish. Brush it with beaten egg and lay the pastry crust over
it, trimming the excess and pressing down the edges. Decorate with
pastry leaves, cut a central cross through which the steam can escape
and brush with beaten egg. Bake for 20–25 minutes, then lower the
oven temperature to 180°C/350°F/Gas 4 and cook for another
20 minutes or so.

Now look, if you think pasties should be bought in a shop with that livid, rather bilious-looking yellow glaze to them that smacks of colouring not egg wash, and a great stodgy rope of pastry around the edge, and if you believe that those doughy lumps with a few disappointing cubes of over-dry meat, turnip, carrot and onion are the real McCoy, let me tell you that the precise reason these pockets of delight are called bridies is because they were originally seen as something simple that a bride would be able to cook for her new husband and enter in her cookery book. You can really do as you will for the filling, just remember that texture is needed somewhere in the equation, so don't mince everything. If, for example, you decide upon crabmeat, add some cubed, softened fennel, a few peas and some cubes of new potato cooked with a hint of saffron. Pasties are a great way of shifting a bit of cold meat – chicken and ham, beef, pork or lamb – but you may, of course, start from scratch and cook the meat with the vegetables in a frying pan.

Forfar Bridies
Welsh Chicken and Leek Pasties

MAKES 8
450g/1lb cooked chicken
  without the skin, roughly
  chopped
55g/2oz butter
whites of 4 leeks, cleaned and
  finely chopped
2 tbsp flat-leaf parsley,
  chopped
3 tbsp redcurrant jelly
225g/8oz cooked potatoes,
  diced
sea salt and black pepper
shortcrust pastry made with
  340g/12oz plain flour and
  170g/6oz unsalted butter
  (see p.140)
beaten egg for glaze

Melt the butter in a pan and add the leeks, cooking them until softened. Add the chicken, parsley, redcurrant jelly and potatoes, season and allow to cool.

Preheat the oven to 180°C/350°F/Gas 4. Roll out the pastry and cut out 8 rounds, each measuring about 15cm/6in across. Put a spoonful of the mixture into the middle of each circle, dampen the edges of the pastry and fold it over to make a half-moon shape. Pinch and crimp the edges to seal. Repeat to make the rest of the pasties.

Glaze the pasties with beaten egg and put them on a greased baking sheet. Bake for 35 minutes or until golden.

Think of this as an exotic Spanish pork pie. Pies are big in Galicia, either stuffed full of fresh shellfish for the returning fishermen, or, like this densely meaty offering, filled with pork, perked up with spicy chorizo and studded with vibrant vegetables. You can make the meat filling up to a day or two in advance if it suits you.

Galician Pork and Sausage Pie

SERVES 8

1kg/2¼lb loin of pork, off the bone, cut into cubes

170g/6oz raw ham or smoked gammon, diced

3 chorizo sausages, the fat rather than the thin version, sliced. I buy organic ones from Swaddles Farm

450g/1lb red and yellow or just red peppers

3 bulbs of fennel

225g/8oz onion, chopped

150ml/5fl oz good olive oil

4 cloves of garlic, finely chopped

200g/7oz tinned whole organic tomatoes

170ml/6fl oz dry white wine

a generous pinch of saffron stamens soaked in a little warm water

1 tsp paprika

handful of flat-leaf parsley, chopped

2 hard-boiled eggs, chopped

sea salt and black pepper

Wine pastry:

400g/13oz flour

sea salt

85g/3oz lard or butter

85g/3oz olive oil

60ml/2fl oz dry white wine

2 eggs

beaten egg for glaze

Seed and slice the peppers. Ruthlessly strip the outer leaves from the fennel bulbs and cut the bulbs vertically into six to eight pieces. Keep the frondy bits.

To make the filling, sauté the onion in some of the oil over a gentle heat, adding the garlic when the onions begin to turn gold. Add the pork and ham or gammon and fry until the meat begins to brown. Add a good glug more of oil and throw in the chunks of chorizo and slices of pepper and fennel. Continue to fry. Add the tomatoes in their juice, chopping them down into the pan as you go, then the wine, saffron, paprika, parsley and seasoning. Cook over a gentle heat for 20 minutes until the pork is cooked through and the liquid has reduced and thickened, then leave to cool for as long as you want.

Make the wine pastry in the food processor. Sift the flour and salt into the bowl with the lard or butter and then add the olive oil, wine and as much of the two eggs as you need to make it cohere and form a paste. Chill in clingfilm for 20 minutes.

Meanwhile, heat the oven to 190°C/375°F/Gas 5 and place a baking sheet on the middle shelf. Roll out two pieces of pastry, one slightly larger than the other, and put the larger one into the pie dish, allowing a little overhang all the way round. Pile the filling into the pie, adding the chopped hard-boiled eggs, then trim the overhang so that you can still fold the edges of the pastry on to the filling. Brush some beaten egg on to the pastry rim, then place the other piece of rolled-out pastry over the pie. Press the edges together with the tines of a fork and trim the pastry to fit the dish. Brush all over with beaten egg and prick the surface at intervals with a fork. Place on the baking sheet and bake for 50 minutes to an hour. Moreish.

So you know about the gammon and spinach of nursery rhyme fame, but perhaps you were not aware that the British don't hold the entire monopoly or panoply of pies to their credit. The French, Greeks, Spanish, Italians and Moroccans all have their own; in fact, does any country not have its version of meat, flesh, fish, fowl or vegetable bound and tightly enclosed in a doughy ball, dumpling, brik, parcel or pie?

This vegetable pie, which is found down through Italy to Calabria and Sicily, is not dissimilar to the famous Ligurian Torta Pasqualina, or Easter Pie, made with artichokes and ricotta.

Torta Rustica con Spinaci
Spinach and Ham Pie

SERVES 6

500g/a generous 1lb of spinach, washed and tough stalks removed

225g/8oz organic vine-ripened tomatoes, skinned and sliced

170g/6oz cooked ham, diced

500g/a generous 1lb of mozzarella di bufala, only good quality will do

sea salt and black pepper

Pastry:

225g/8oz flour

50g/scant 2oz sugar

sea salt

grated zest of an organic lemon

110g/4oz unsalted butter

3 egg yolks

beaten egg for glaze

To make the pastry, mix together the flour, sugar, salt and lemon zest, then rub in small pieces of cold butter. Add the egg yolks as quickly as you can and work until the mixture coheres into a ball. You may need to add a little cold water.

Preheat the oven to 230°C/450°F/Gas 8. Cook the wet spinach briefly, just until it wilts, adding no water to the pan but stirring to prevent it burning or sticking. Tip the spinach into a colander and press down hard with the back of a wooden spoon to remove all the water.

Divide the dough into two-thirds and one-third. Take a 23cm/9in tart tin with a removable base, grease and line it with the rolled-out larger piece of pastry. Spread the squeezed-out spinach evenly over the pastry base. Lay the slices of tomato on top in slightly overlapping concentric circles, then sprinkle with ham and mozzarella and season well. A hint of nutmeg is a good addition.

Roll out the remaining third of the dough and cover the filling with it, sealing the edges with the tines of a fork dipped into cold water. Prick the top all over with a fork and brush with beaten egg. Cook for 10 minutes before turning the oven temperature down to 150°C/300°F/Gas 2 and baking for another 30 minutes or until the pie is crisped, golden and smelling cooked. Remove from the oven and leave for at least 10 minutes before eating.

Various forms of this pie are found all over the Mediterranean, where it is traditionally served at Easter. The French have their own version, Tourte de Pâques, the pastry made with olive oil, but in Italy it is made with filo pastry in a springform tin, so it emerges from its chrysalis of tin fully fledged, seamed with crocus yellow and green, lactic and salt with ricotta and Parmesan cheese. If you can't find Swiss chard, you can use spinach, though half spinach, half artichoke hearts is a combination devoutly to be wished. A beautiful centrepiece to a lunch that you can make the day before you want to eat it, then reheat in a low oven to crisp the pastry. The torta is best eaten at room temperature or warm.

La Torta Pasqualina

SERVES 8

1.8kg/4lb Swiss chard
120ml/4fl oz olive oil
2 cloves of garlic, peeled and bruised
3 tbsp chopped marjoram
450g/1lb fresh ricotta
55g/2oz Parmesan cheese, freshly grated
55g/2oz unsalted butter
6 eggs
sea salt and black pepper
340g/12oz filo pastry

Tear the washed leaves from the chard stalks and cut both into strips. Plunge the stalks into a pan of boiling salted water and add the leaves after 5 minutes. Cook until they are both tender, then drain and press out all the excess water. Pour a couple of tablespoons of the olive oil into a frying pan and add the garlic and marjoram. The moment you scent the garlic, remove it, add the chard to the pan and sauté it for 5 minutes, stirring all the time. Season with lots of coarsely ground black pepper and leave it to cool. Put the ricotta in a bowl and break it up thoroughly with a fork.

Preheat the oven to 180°C/350°F/Gas 4. Grease a 25cm/10in springform tin with a little olive oil and fit 10 sheets of filo pastry, one on top of the other, so that the edges droop over the sides of the tin. Brush each sheet with olive oil as you go, and keep the filo under a damp cloth – it dries out and tears more quickly than you'd believe possible. Spread the chard over the bottom, then add the crumbled ricotta and half the Parmesan with a generous scrunch of black pepper. Shape five hollows around the edge of the filling and place a knob of butter in each, then carefully break an egg into each hollow.

Sprinkle the rest of the Parmesan over the top, and cover with another 10 sheets of filo, oiling each one as you go. Turn the overhang into the centre and roll it like a cigar to form a ridge at the edge of the pie, then brush the top liberally with olive oil. Bake for 30 minutes, then turn the heat up to 200°C/400°F/Gas 6 and bake for a further 20 minutes to crisp the top. Let the torta cool in the tin before sliding it on to a plate.

More often than not this delectable dish is made with olive oil pastry, so by all means use it for this pie, but here I've used a buttery pastry with a slug of oil – much easier to work without it collapsing into bits. Don't stint on the artichokes, the briney ones are not right for this dish. Either cook them yourself – perfect at the beginning of the season around Easter when the first little violet-eared, mossy green artichokes are in the markets – or use a first-class jar like Seggiano's charcoal-grilled artichokes in olive oil. A wonderful, extravagantly elegant dish for a special picnic or al fresco lunch in early summer, but the appeal to me is that cusp of the season thing, when spring vegetables are shrieking with newness, greenness, fecundity.

Tourte de Pâques

SERVES 8

450g/1lb spinach, washed and stalked

400g/13oz jar artichoke bottoms

4 tbsp extra virgin olive oil

1 onion, very finely diced

1 clove garlic, very finely chopped

6 eggs, boiled for 6 minutes

salt and black pepper

Pastry:

450g/1lb plain flour

225g/8oz unsalted butter

2 eggs, beaten

3 tbsp extra virgin olive oil

½ tsp sea salt

To make the pastry, rub the flour and butter together until crumbly, then mix in the eggs, olive oil and salt, adding a little cold water if the mixture is too crumbly. Wrap the ball of pastry in clingfilm and put it in the fridge for at least 30 minutes.

Heat a tablespoon of olive oil in a large frying pan and add the chopped onion, cooking it over a medium heat for about 5 minutes until softened. Add the garlic and cook for another couple of minutes. Tip into a large bowl, then add another slug of olive oil to the pan and cook the spinach in batches for 3–4 minutes until wilted. Put it in a colander to drain. Heat a little more oil in the pan, add the artichokes and fry them for 3–4 minutes. Mix the spinach and artichokes into the onion and garlic and season well. Leave the mixture to cool.

Divide the ball of pastry into two, one piece slightly larger than the other. Roll out the larger disc of pastry and place it in an oiled 25cm/10in tart tin, with a removable base. Patch the pastry as you see fit, it rarely makes it in one into the tin. Spoon in the filling, then halve the eggs and push them, cut side up, into the filling. Brush the rim of pastry with oil, fit the smaller, rolled-out circle on top, crimp the edges and brush with a little more olive oil.

Bake for 30–35 minutes at 200°C/400°F/Gas 6. The filling is already cooked, so it's only the pastry you need to watch. Let the pie cool to room temperature and remove it from the tart tin to serve.

It's a myth that hot water crust pastry is impossible or even difficult to make; equally, the idea that the pork pie should be a shop-bought thing of dubiously bright pink meat, with an inner layer of slimy-white, half-raw pastry with a slick of salty jelly on top. It is remarkably easy to make a delicious pork pie of your own, either individual ones shaped around a glass or ring, or a full-scale model shaped around a springform or biscuit tin if you don't have the requisite almond-shaped clipped mould. The butcher will mince the pork and the bacon for you, the rest is hardly a culinary challenge. But the result is stunning and makes a deeply impressive picnic.

Somerset Pork Pie with Cider and Apples

SERVES 6
450g/1lb pork, coarsely minced
450g/1lb pork, cubed
85g/3oz bacon bits, minced
110g/4oz onion, chopped
90ml/3fl oz good strong dry cider
½ tbsp sea salt
1 tsp freshly ground black pepper
½ tsp freshly ground mace
110g/4oz good tart eating apple, peeled and chopped
2 tbsp fresh sage, chopped

Hot water crust pastry:
250g/8½ oz lard
300ml/10½fl oz boiling water
560g/1¼lb plain flour
½ tsp sea salt
beaten egg for glaze

Chop the lard into bits and melt it in the boiling water. Pour it into a large bowl containing the flour and salt and work the warm paste into a ball. You will need to roll three-quarters of it out for the base and sides of the pie and the final quarter for the lid.

Build the crust by placing the tin inside the circle of pastry you have rolled out and moulding the walls around the tin. Then to help the crust keep its shape, wrap a sheet of greaseproof paper around the pastry walls and tie string around it, one piece 2.5cm/1in or so from the bottom and one 2.5cm/1in or so from the top.

Remove the tin and fill the crust with the filling ingredients which you have mulched together in the bowl with your fingers. Press the filling in so that it is packed tightly right to the top, then cover with the circle of pastry and crimp the edges with your fingers. Brush all over with beaten egg and cut a hole in the top for the steam to escape before you bake it.

Put in the oven at 200°C/400°F/Gas 6 for 30 minutes to firm up the pastry and let it begin to colour, then turn the heat down to 160°C/325°F/Gas 3 and leave for about 2 hours for the meat to cook through. Keep checking the lid of the pastry and protect it with a sheet of greaseproof paper if it begins to colour too deeply too quickly. Remove the pie from the oven and take off the greaseproof and string. Brush the sides of the pie with beaten egg and return to the oven to colour for 10 minutes. Finish with jellied stock as for the Melton Mowbray pie on page 60.

This is the journeyman version of the Somerset Pork Pie, but for those who feel faint hearted about hot water crust pastry, this is the definition of simple. It goes without saying that this is a dish of substance, something for the ravening teenage maw of hunger or that children and adults will crave after a windy walk on a chill day, when less is most certainly not more.

Sausage and Apple Pie

SERVES 6–8

450g/1lb best organic pork sausage meat

2 tbsp fresh sage leaves, chopped

2 large Cox's or similar sharp-flavoured eating apples, peeled and thinly sliced

sea salt, black pepper and nutmeg

450g/1lb puff pastry (see p.141)

beaten egg for glaze

Preheat the oven to 220°C/425°F/Gas 7. Roll out half the pastry and use it to line a 23cm/9in pie plate. Place a layer of half the sausage meat mixed with the chopped sage over the pastry base. Cover with the thinly sliced apples. Season well, then top with the rest of the sausage meat mixture. Roll out the rest of the pastry and cover the pie, brushing the edges of the base with the beaten egg before sticking and crimping the crust to them. Cut a cross through the centre of the pastry so the steam can escape while cooking. Put the pie in the fridge for half an hour.

Brush the pie with beaten egg and put it in the oven on a heated baking tray for 15 minutes. Turn the heat down to 180°C/350°F/Gas 4 and cook for a further 30–40 minutes until puffed up and golden. Use the point of a skewer to make sure the apple is cooked through. Leave for 10 minutes before serving.

What you need is a green confetti of herbs strewn over this light summer dish, so use poetic licence – what's available, what matches, what's in your garden. Tarragon and parsley, parsley and basil, chervil and chives or sage, thyme and parsley would all make equally good bedfellows.

Green Herb and Bacon Pie

SERVES 6–8
450g/1lb green back bacon rashers, the rinds snipped off
450g/1lb white of leek, finely chopped
225g/8oz spinach, finely chopped
1 bunch of watercress, finely chopped
a handful of flat-leaf parsley, finely chopped
2 eggs
4 tbsp Jersey double cream
120ml/4fl oz good jellied chicken stock, cold
sea salt and black pepper
shortcrust pastry made with 170g/6oz flour and 85g/3oz unsalted butter (see p.140)
beaten egg for glaze

Preheat the oven to 180°C/350°F/Gas 4. Line a 1.5-litre/3-pint pie dish with half the rashers and top with the leeks mixed with the spinach, watercress and parsley. Beat the two eggs with the cream and pour them over the vegetable and herb mixture, season, then add the jellied stock. Lay the remaining rashers over the top and shroud in pastry in the usual way. Brush with beaten egg and bake until the pie is golden brown, about an hour.

Bring back the bunny. This tender prewar dish has been almost totally eschewed from our present-day repertoire. Indeed, getting hold of wild rabbits has become an increasingly specialist operation if you don't shoot them yourself, so few butchers are there who stock them, even in the country. The tame sort are some kind of a substitute. They are usually very tender, but you will lose on the taste front what you gain on the tenderness. Just remember what a natural affinity the little cottontails have with bacon and prunes, and you will arrive in perfect rabbit piedom with ease.

The Norwich dealer I first went to as a wet-behind-the-ears but keen game cook, bore a legendary inscription chalked on to his shop window. This, after all, was in the days of *Watership Down*. 'You've read the book, you've seen the film, now try the pie.'

Rabbit Pie

SERVES 6–8

2 rabbits, jointed, with their
   livers and kidneys
a dozen prunes d'Agen
apple juice or cider
2 large onions, sliced
6 sage leaves
2 or 3 rashers of unsmoked
   back bacon, thickly cut
2 or 3 hard-boiled eggs
a large bunch of flat-leaf
   parsley, chopped
290ml/10fl oz good jellied
   chicken stock
sea salt and black pepper
shortcrust pastry made with
   225g/8oz flour and 110g/4oz
   unsalted butter (see p.140)
   or puff pastry (p.141),
   depending on whether
   you're going rich or poor
beaten egg for glaze

Soak the prunes in apple juice or cider and cook gently. Leave to cool, then carefully remove the stones and set aside the liquid.

Put the rabbit pieces in a large, heavy-bottomed casserole with the sliced onions and sage. Add the apple juice or cider used for cooking the prunes, bring to the boil, then simmer very gently for 30 minutes. Strip the meat from the bone as soon as it isn't too hot to handle, then leave it to cool. Meanwhile, cook the bacon and snip into chunky strips.

Preheat the oven to 200°C/400°F/Gas 6. Finely chop and season the rabbit livers and kidneys and, using a tiny teaspoon, stuff this mixture into the prunes. Put the pieces of rabbit and bacon into a pie dish with slices of hard-boiled egg, a good handful of chopped parsley and the stuffed prunes. Season well before pouring in the cold chicken stock. Cover with the pastry, cut a cross with a sharp knife in the top and glaze with beaten egg.

Cook for about an hour, turning the heat down after the first 20 minutes to 180°C/350°F/Gas 4. I think this is best left until the next day and then served cold, but the choice is yours.

Cottage Pie with yesterday's beef, Shepherd's Pie with lamb. The classic Monday supper after a Sunday roast, if there's anyone left who still enjoys the rituals of a proper Sunday lunch. Well I do for one, and cannot imagine the paucity of pleasure endured by those who don't see this arcane ritual for what it really is: for its not insignificant role in holding the fabric of our society together, its indigenous nature – the English have always had a reputation for being skilful roasters – and its bringing the whole family and friends to the table in this age where such commonsense is seen as a curious anachronism. So why buy a joint that will only suffice for Sunday lunch? Well, I guess in this era of instant gratification, food faddism and arugula-with-everything, many people have never considered leftover dishes to be a part of their culinary landscape. And this, the most creative form of cooking.

Shepherd's Pie, Cottage Pie

SERVES 6

675g/1½lb or thereabouts minced lamb
1 large onion, chopped
1 large carrot, finely chopped
3 cloves of garlic, chopped
3–4 tbsp olive oil
1 tbsp tomato purée
150–270ml/5–10fl oz yesterday's gravy
150–270ml/5–10fl oz red wine (you need 425ml/15fl oz liquid including the gravy and wine)
Worcestershire sauce
Tabasco
sea salt and black pepper
1kg/2¼lb potatoes, peeled, boiled and mashed with milk and a generous quantity of butter
more butter

Stew the onion, carrot and garlic gently in the olive oil until softened, then raise the heat and add the minced lamb, turning it so that it browns all over. Mix in the tomato, wine and gravy – in my case made with meat juices, the meat roasted on a layer of sliced onions which caramelize, rendering the gravy intensely flavoured and coloured, and cooked down with a splash of red wine and the water the vegetables have been cooked in. Continue to simmer very gently for 15 minutes or so while you are cooking and mashing the potatoes.

Preheat the oven to 200°C/400°F/Gas 6. Five minutes before you finish cooking the mince, shake in some Worcestershire sauce and Tabasco to taste. Keep tasting, rather than being heavy handed and overdoing the spice and heat at the beginning. When you have the flavour you want, decant the mince into a gratin or pie dish and cover with mashed potato. Ruffle the surface with a fork before dotting with butter.

Cook for 10 minutes to get the potatoes browning, then turn the temperature down to 180°C/350°F/Gas 4 and continue to cook for 45 minutes. You can bake Shepherd's Pie longer and slower if it suits you, but still start with the 10-minute hot blast.

This slow-simmered ragu – a picture of contentment on the stove top as it gently coalesces, meat with milk, tomato with wine, vegetable with nutmeg and bay leaf, blipping at a bare bubble for its three hour melt-down to oily rich perfection – is the basis of my Italian Cottage Pie. Thoroughly un-English a rendering as it is, this is a wonderful variant that is always worth the making extra ragu for.

Italian Cottage Pie

SERVES 6

1kg/2¼lb minced beef chuck or similar, with a goodly amount of fat

3–4 tbsp olive oil

a knob of butter

2 large onions, finely chopped

3 sticks of celery, strung and finely chopped

3 carrots, finely diced

3 or 4 cloves of garlic, finely chopped

240ml/8½fl oz milk

240ml/8½fl oz white wine

2 x 400g/13oz tins of organic whole plum tomatoes

sea salt, black pepper, bay leaves and nutmeg

1kg/2¼lb potatoes, boiled and mashed with milk and lashings of butter

Warm the oil and butter in a heavy cast-iron pot, add the onion, celery and carrots with a sprinkling of salt to help the vegetables release their juices and sauté gently until they soften. Add the garlic and continue cooking for another couple of minutes. Add the beef and a little more salt, grind over some black pepper and stir until the meat has just lost its raw pink look. Add a couple of bay leaves and the milk and simmer gently for 10 minutes until the meat has absorbed a lot of the milk. Odd you may think, but adding milk to the meat has a mellowing effect, cutting through the acidic bite of the tomatoes you will add later. Grate in a suspicion of nutmeg, then add the wine and let it simmer into the meat for 10–15 minutes before adding the tins of tomatoes and chopping them into the meat. Cook at the laziest, most slatternly of simmers for 3 hours. You really can leave the pot unattended for that long, so don't be disgruntled by the length of time it takes, you don't need to watch over it. Go to the movies, to bed, to work, read a book… and then give it a stir, you will notice the oil has turned tomatoey red and separated. Great. Correct the seasoning and you are ready to go.

Tip the ragu into a pie dish and lash on the mash. At some stage of the proceedings you will have remembered to turn the oven on to 200°C/400°F/Gas 6 to preheat. Bake at this temperature for the first 10–15 minutes, then turn down to 180°C/350°F/Gas 4 for a further 45 minutes until crusted brown and bubbling. Serve with a simple green salad of cos lettuce, or some buttery petits pois.

A gorgeous and unusual Greek dish, which you can serve with a chicory and watercress salad, pepped up with some coriander and a good, nutty dressing.

Noisettes of Lamb in Vine Leaves and Filo Pastry

SERVES 4

8 lamb noisettes, 2.5cm/1in thick, trimmed of fat, leaving the 'eye' of lean meat
8 large vine leaves, soaked as instructions on the jar
3 cloves of garlic, finely chopped
1 tsp oregano or marjoram
sea salt
4 sheets filo pastry
melted butter
egg white
1 lemon

Marinade:

6 tbsp olive oil
2 tbsp lemon juice
120ml/4fl oz red wine
black pepper

Put all the marinade ingredients into a bowl and throw in the lamb noisettes, leaving them to absorb everything for an hour. Then drain them and pat them dry with kitchen paper.

Preheat the oven to 220°C/425°F/Gas 7. Cut the sheets of filo in half lengthwise and brush them with melted butter. Season the lamb noisettes with sea salt, sprinkle with a little garlic and oregano and wrap each one in a vine leaf. Place a piece of lamb at the narrow end of a filo strip, flip over the sides and roll up the parcel. Seal each end with a dab of egg white on your pastry brush. Make the rest of the parcels this way and brush each one with melted butter.

Place the parcels on a preheated baking sheet you've whacked in the oven and cook for 10 minutes for pink lamb. Alternatively, you can deep fry the parcels in hot oil for 4–5 minutes until golden. Serve with quarters of lemon and salad.

The famous Russian fish pie: a glorious puffed pillow of pastry enveloping its secrets – wild salmon, dill, mushrooms, hard-boiled eggs and, in its traditional incarnation, kasha, or buckwheat, which has first been roasted. This is a party piece, but you can use a salmon you have cooked and made inroads into the day before, and you can pre-cook the rice or kasha.

Kulebiaka or Salmon Pie

SERVES 6

675–700g/about 1½lb filleted wild salmon, cooked or raw
225g/8oz unsalted butter
225g/8oz shallots or onions, chopped
225g/8oz chestnut or organic mushrooms, coarsely chopped
juice of a lemon
170g/6oz brown rice or kasha
425ml/15fl oz water or chicken stock
2 tbsp fresh dill, chopped
2 tbsp flat-leaf parsley, chopped
3 hard-boiled eggs, sliced
sea salt, black pepper, nutmeg
puff pastry made with 450g/1lb flour (see p.141)
beaten egg yolk for glaze

If the salmon is raw, cut it carefully into 60mm/¼in slices, then fry them briefly in 85g/3oz of the butter. They should still have a raw colour. Gently sauté half the onions or shallots in a little more of the butter until softened and golden, then add the mushrooms and cook for a further 5 minutes. Spritz with the lemon juice and season. Fry the rest of the onion gently in a little more butter until soft, then add the rice or kasha and stir to coat each grain before adding 425ml/15fl oz of water or chicken stock. Simmer gently, adding more liquid if you need to. When the rice or kasha is cooked, add the dill, parsley, salt, pepper and nutmeg.

Preheat the oven to 200°C/400°F/Gas 6. Roll out half the pastry into an oblong and place it on a baking sheet. Put half the rice or kasha on top of it, leaving 2.5cm/1in uncovered all the way round the edge. Add the sliced salmon, followed by the sliced hard-boiled eggs and lastly the mushroom mixture. Cover with the rest of the rice or kasha.

Roll out the rest of the pastry. Brush the rim of the lower piece of pastry with beaten egg and lay the second layer on top, pressing it down to seal the edges together. Turn over the rim to double it and mark it all the way around with the tines of a fork. Decorate in any shape or form you like – I make pastry fish.

Cut a cross in the centre of the pie through which the steam can escape, brush the top with the beaten egg and bake for an hour. If the pastry is colouring too quickly, cover it with buttered greaseproof paper. Just before serving, melt the rest of the butter and pour it through the central hole.

I think a bowl of soured cream served alongside the kulebiaka, with or without some more finely chopped dill, is a great addition.

Who ever heard of a perfect pairing of salmon with ginger with currants? It is not just odd, it is unappealing. But if I were to tell you that this is a match for life – one that is going to endure the test of time and outlive food faddery and fandango – and beg you to try it, then you might just go ahead and you might agree. When I first ate it, cooked by my number one culinary hero George Perry-Smith, it was a revelation. And it has another glory – that of looking as beautiful and difficult to make as you could imagine, but without actually being so. Just make sure you buy wild salmon. Farmed salmon is sacrilege, a sop to the supermarket mentality that the punters have to have everything they want all of the time.

Salmon Baked in Pastry with Ginger and Currants

SERVES 6

1kg/2¼lb piece of wild salmon, cut from the tail end, skinned and filleted (a good fishmonger will do this for you)

3 orbs of ginger in syrup, drained and diced very small

30g/1oz currants

110g/4oz unsalted butter, softened

sea salt and black pepper

shortcrust pastry made with 450g/1lb flour and 225g/8oz unsalted butter (see p.140)

beaten egg for glaze

Preheat the oven to 230°C/450°F/Gas 8. Check that there are no bones remaining in the pieces of salmon and season on both sides. Using a fork, incorporate the diced ginger and currants into the softened butter. Spread half the mixture over the bottom salmon fillet, place the top fillet over it and spread it with the rest of the butter mixture.

Roll out the pastry and place the salmon on it. Join the edges of the pastry into a parcel, sealing them with a little milk and making sure they aren't lumpy. Brush with the egg yolk, place on an ungreased baking sheet and bake in the oven for 30 minutes.

If you are remotely worried that it might not be quite cooked, and the thickness of salmon does vary, insert a skewer right the way through the fish. If it goes through easily, it's a done deal. Remove from the oven to rest for 5 minutes before cutting it into slices and serving with its greatest accompaniment: Sauce Messine.

Sauce Messine:

570ml/1 pint single cream

2 egg yolks

2 tsp French mustard

2 tsp plain flour

110g/4oz butter, softened

juice of an organic lemon

half a small onion, very finely chopped

a small bunch of mixed fresh herbs, tarragon, parsley, chervil, dill, chopped

Sauce Messine

Swirl all the ingredients together in a blender until green. Heat the sauce through gently in the top of a double boiler until thickened, stirring constantly. Serve in a warm bowl, accompanied by either a cucumber salad or some Jersey new potatoes and stewed fresh peas.

Just no tomatoes in it please, and no cheese in the sauce and no quarters of eggs boiled overly hard, with their grainy yellow planets of solidified yolk surrounded by an orbit of black. This is comfort food of the highest order – it can be peasant simple or luscious luxurious. You can use one simple fish, cut out the leeks and dill and white wine, add parsley, hold the scallops and throw in some prawns. You can make a nursery food equivalent – still the kind of dish from which you're impelled to scrape the cooling leftovers, the crusting morsels of potato that cling recalcitrantly to the dish and are as attractive, curiously, when cold and thick set as when piping, scalding, buttery hot.

Cod, Smoked Haddock and Scallop Pie

SERVES 6

1kg/2¼lb cod or unsmoked haddock, skinned and filleted

225g/8oz or so natural smoked haddock

8 or 9 scallops with large commas of coral, cleaned and the white discs sliced in two, the corals left whole or sliced if large enough

290–425ml/10–15fl oz milk

55g/2oz unsalted butter

30g/1oz plain flour

1 bay leaf, nutmeg

a large glass of white wine, or better still vermouth

the white part of three leeks, cleaned and cut into rings

1kg/2¼lb potatoes, peeled, cooked and mashed with butter and milk

a handful of fresh dill, chopped

sea salt and black pepper

Put the unsmoked piece of fish in a gratin dish, pour over the milk and cook in the oven for 15 minutes. It may not be cooked right through when you remove it, but that doesn't matter. Remove any bones and flake the fish in large chunks into the gratin dish you're going to cook it in, reserving the poaching milk. Meanwhile, cover the smoked haddock in boiling water for 10 minutes. Drain the water off and flake the haddock into the gratin dish. Make a roux with the butter and flour, then add the hot poaching milk, bay leaf and a suspicion of grated nutmeg and whisk into a smooth sauce. Add the wine or vermouth, cooking it down for at least 10 minutes. Season well with black pepper, but go easy on the salt as smoked fish carries a lot of it. Steam the leeks until tender and add them to the fish.

Preheat the oven to 180°C/350°F/Gas 4. Put the raw scallops and the coral in with the fish, then strew the handful of dill into the sauce and pour it over the fish. Cover with mashed potato, ruffle the top with a fork and dot with butter. Place on a baking tray and consign to the heat for about 30 minutes. The sauce often erupts through the potato like a geyser and courses down the sides, which is part of the charm of the finished offering. One of the few dishes that really should be brought to the table nuclear hot.

Here the bacon acts as a wrapper, taking the place of pastry in a wonderfully creamy, garlicky pie baked in a terrine. A lovely winter lunch or supper dish.

Tourte de Pommes de Terre au Lard
Potato and Bacon Pie

SERVES 6
400g/13oz potatoes
30g/1oz unsalted butter
2 medium onions, sliced
85g/3oz organic streaky
  bacon, diced
2 cloves of garlic, crushed
  with the back of a knife
270ml/9fl oz double cream
5 egg yolks
7 or 8 rashers green back
  bacon, rinds snipped off
sea salt and black pepper

Cook the potatoes in their skins until they're soft, then drain and peel. Cut into thick slices and set aside. Heat the butter in a frying pan, throw in the onions and stir them over a slow heat for 10 minutes until they have wilted and are beginning to change colour. Add the diced streaky bacon and the garlic and continue to cook for a further 3 minutes or so, then pour in the cream. Let it boil for a minute, then transfer everything to a bowl and leave to cool.

Heat the oven to 180°C/350°F/Gas 4. When the onion and bacon mixture is nearly cold, stir in the egg yolks and season with pepper, then add the sliced potatoes. Line the bottom and sides of a 900g/2lb terrine with the bacon rashers and scrape in the mixture. Cover with a layer of greaseproof paper. Put the dish in a roasting tin and pour in hot water to come half way up the sides of the terrine.

Bake the pie in the oven for 50–60 minutes, until fairly firm to the touch. Turn out on to a plate and serve piping hot, with nothing more than a well-dressed green salad.

This is rice based like the Italian tortas on the next page, but here the rice is cooked before it is introduced to the other ingredients of this delectably rich Greek pie. If you baulk at the idea of making your own filo pastry, don't. I mean don't baulk, it's as easy as ordinary pastry. The shop-bought version you're used to seeing in boxes is too fragile for this kind of pie; the homemade version is thicker. If you do chicken out, just make your normal shortcrust pastry with half butter, half olive oil and roll it out as thin as you can without it sticking and overstretching.

Feta, Rice and Yoghurt Pie

SERVES 6–8
340g/12oz feta
200g/7oz carnaroli or arborio rice
310g/11oz Greek yoghurt
570ml/1 pint Jersey milk
1 tbsp olive oil
a bunch of spring onions, finely chopped
30g/1oz dill, finely chopped
3 eggs
a handful of sesame seeds
sea salt and black pepper

Homemade filo:
1kg/2¼lb white 00 pasta flour
1 dsrtsp sea salt
about 250ml/8½fl oz water
1 tbsp white wine vinegar
4 tbsp extra virgin olive oil
beaten egg for glaze

To make the pastry, sift the flour and salt into a large bowl, make a well in the centre and add the water and vinegar. Work the dough until it is smooth, then begin to add the olive oil, a little at a time, kneading thoroughly until the dough is stretchy and shiny and the oil has been absorbed. Wrap in clingfilm and refrigerate until cold.

Preheat the oven to 180°C/350°F/Gas 4. Grease a 25cm/10in springform tin with butter. Put the milk, olive oil and a little sea salt in a large, heavy-bottomed pan and bring to scalding point, then stir in the rice. Cover the pan and simmer for 20 minutes.

Put the yoghurt and feta in a food processor and mix to a smooth paste. Add the spring onions and dill and blitz for a nano-second. Add the eggs to the feta mixture, one at a time down the feed tube, then scrape the mixture out of the processor and into the rice. Stir to amalgamate.

Roll the filo out into two long thin sheets in a pasta machine, or by hand, as thin as you can. One sheet should be a little larger than the second. Line the tin with the larger piece, don't worry about the overhang at this stage. Then scrape the cooled mixture into the tin, and level the top. Cover the filling with the second piece of pastry. Fold in any short edges towards the centre of the pie and cut the longer ones off. Brush the rim of the bottom layer of pastry with a little milk or water and seal the top to the bottom. Brush the surface of the pie with beaten egg, prick the surface all over with a fork and scatter over a handful of sesame seeds. Bake for about an hour and eat while still warm.

My friend and brilliant fellow cook George Morley originally told me about the great Anna del Conte's Torta di Porri, which is disarmingly simple to make, yet looks like a suitably complex party piece. I've added my own touches, like some lemon zest and juice and a longer soaking time to ensure the starch in the carnaroli rice has ample opportunity to begin leaching into the olive oil and the rice to soften and swell. Otherwise proceed as follows. This dish is best served warm, when the texture and flavour has set, but Anna del Conte also makes it a day in advance and serves it at room temperature,

The porcini version makes a spectacularly bosky, musky torta. I would say only this: do not dilute the strong-scented beauty of the porcini with any other fungi; if you can't lay your hands on enough, just make a smaller torta.

La Torta di Porri

Lightly beat the eggs and put them into a bowl with the leeks, rice, 200ml/7fl oz of the oil, two teaspoons of salt, plenty of black pepper and the Parmesan. Add the grated lemon zest and juice. Add the basil that you have stripped from its stalks and torn into smallish pieces, then mix everything together with your hands. Set the bowl aside for 3–4 hours, the longer the better, mixing everything around every so often to keep it lubricated.

Preheat the oven to 180°C/350°F/Gas 4. Oil a 25cm/10in springform tin, then pour the rest of the oil into a small bowl. Carefully unfold the filo pastry – it tears easily – and remove one leaf at a time, keeping the rest under a damp tea towel so it doesn't dry out. Lay one leaf over the tin and work it down into the bottom to the base, allowing the extra to hang over one side. Don't worry if it tears a little. Brush it gently all over with a little olive oil. Lay the next leaf of filo just overlapping the first, and covering a further bit of the tin, and oil in the same way. Do the same with another two leaves of filo, then tip the filling into the tin and spread it out to flatten the top. Fold the overhanging pieces of filo over the mixture into the middle of the tin and brush with oil. If you don't have enough, add another four leaves to cover brushed in the same way. Cut them with scissors to fit inside the tin and fold the overlap over so that it makes a little ridge around the outside of the tin. Bake for 45–50 minutes on a preheated baking tray. Let the pie cool out of the oven for 10 minutes, then unclip and remove the tin and turn the torte upside down on to the baking tray, putting it back into the oven for a further 5–10 minutes to crisp up. Cool until it is just warm before eating.

SERVES 6–8

1.2kg/2½lb leeks, washed thoroughly, green parts cut away and white parts cut into very thin discs
6 large organic eggs
140g/5oz carnaroli rice
290ml/10fl oz extra virgin olive oil
9 tbsp Parmesan cheese, freshly grated
zest from 1 organic lemon and the juice of half
a bunch of fresh basil
sea salt and freshly ground black pepper
225–255g/8–9oz filo pastry

La Torta di Zucchini

Use 450g/1lb of courgettes, sliced into exceptionally fine discs, and proceed as above.

La Torta di Porcini

Chop the fungi thinly and then into small pieces and use flat-leaf parsley instead of basil. Take care not to break up the delicate shards of porcini when you mix the ingredients with your fingers.

This is a simple, rustic, laidback, loose-leaf, leaning tower of a pie. The goodies are stacked in pale, flecked strata on each floor of filo, wonkily and perilously perched as you build up and up in what is at most an unskilled assembly job, brickless, mortarless, sideless, but still the definition of a pie.

Layered Ricotta and Feta

SERVES 6–8

500g/a generous 1lb ricotta, fresh if you can get it or in tubs

500g/a generous 1lb good sheep's milk feta

6 large organic eggs

8 tbsp best olive oil, plus some extra for brushing

2 tbsp fresh dill, chopped

2 tbsp fresh mint, chopped

1kg/2¼lb filo pastry

55–85g/2–3oz unsalted butter, melted

500ml/18fl oz milk

2 organic eggs

sea salt and black pepper

Preheat the oven to 200°C/400°F/Gas 6. Whisk the six eggs for the filling together in a large bowl, then add the ricotta, sieving it in for lightness, the feta, which needs crumbling and then whisking in, and 4 tablespoons of oil. Stir in the fresh herbs and season cautiously as feta is so salty.

Brush a large baking sheet with olive oil before laying down your first leaf of filo. Keep the rest of the filo under a damp cloth throughout the process otherwise it dries and tears. Brush with melted butter and add another sheet of filo. Add a layer of the mixture, about 1cm/a scant ½in thick, bringing it right to the edge of the filo. Add another two sheets of oiled filo as before, and the same again of the mixture. Repeat this until your last storey of mixture, then add the penthouse roof of a double layer of filo, this time brushing both layers with melted butter.

Cut a diamond pattern into the filo roof, then beat together the milk, any leftover butter and oil, and two eggs. Gently sluice the liquid over the top of the tower. Let it rest and absorb for 15 minutes, then whack the pie into the hot oven for 8 minutes before turning the temperature down to 150°C/300°F/Gas 2 and baking it for another 20 minutes, or until golden and swollen. Best eaten warm, but you'd guessed that already. A delightfully untemperamental and accommodating sort of Saturday lunchtime dish.

I lifted this from Theodore Kyriakou's lovely book *Real Greek Food*. His recipes are the antithesis of the cliché of Greek holiday food: tepid, oily moussaka and chips and the daily Greek salad that after the third or fourth day does somehow lose its edge and freshness and make the diner wilt. This dish is from Alexandroupoli, the last major Greek city on the way to Turkey, a part of the world that's famous for its buttery pastries. Mmmm.

Cheese Triangles

SERVES 6–8

100g/3½oz Greek feta

100g/3½oz Kaseri or very mature Cheddar. I like Montgomery for its strength of character

100g/3½oz Graviera or mature Gruyère, Beaufort is great

4 organic eggs

3 heaped tbsp fresh mint leaves, chopped

grated nutmeg

freshly ground black pepper

500g/1lb 2oz filo pastry

100g/3½oz unsalted butter, melted

500ml/18fl oz full-cream milk

100g/3½oz cold unsalted butter

Preheat the oven to 180°C/350°F/Gas 4. Grate all the cheeses into a mixing bowl. Add two of the eggs and using a hand blender or food processor, purée the mixture. Add the chopped mint, black pepper and a great deal more than you normally would of grated nutmeg, then mix well. Eschew the salt, there is enough in the cheeses.

Take two sheets of filo, brush one liberally with melted butter, and lay the other exactly on top. Cut this sandwich into strips of about 5 x 20cm/2 x 8in. Put a tablespoon of the cheese filling in the centre of a strip, about 2.5cm/1in from the end. Fold one corner over in a triangle to cover the mixture, fold in the edges about 60mm/¼in, then continue turning over the triangle until you reach the end of the filo strip, buttering it well with each turn. Continue making the pastries until you have finished up all the cheese mixture and place them on an oiled baking tray with a rim.

Beat the milk with the two remaining eggs in a bowl and pour the liquid over the pastry triangles. Leave the pastries to stand uncovered at room temperature until all the liquid has been absorbed. Place one small knob of butter on each triangle and bake in the oven until they are golden, about 35–40 minutes. Theodore recommends eating them with just a purée of aubergines or red peppers as they are so rich.

Versatile, child's play, surprise – these meltingly salt-sweet, crisp-gooey purses of suspended flavour and texture are all the above and more. I like the sculptural element brought to them by getting everyone to construct their own little Fort Knoxes of full-on flavour. I also like the fact that initially you think, 'what a fiddle', but then realize, as you start crumbling cheese, pressing spinach and brushing filo, that the preparation elicits its own satisfaction, even before the hot, crisp morsels are bitten into and savoured with a long, chilled glass of something good. I like to make half blue cheese and half feta parcels. It ups the surprise element and they contrast beautifully. Just keep them at opposite ends of the baking sheet and then put them on separate dishes when they're cooked. I am being deliberately vague about numbers and quantity here. They can be served as a bonne bouche, starter or light lunch. Try the following amounts, which should, according to your manual dexterity and perception of small parcel, give you 15–20 parcels.

Feta or Roquefort and Spinach Parcels

MAKES 15–20
450g/1lb spinach, washed and cooked just until it wilts in the residue of water
1 packet of sheep's milk feta
the same weight of Roquefort or a good blue cheese such as Cashel Blue or Fourme d'Ambert
a little nutmeg or cayenne, sea salt and black pepper
olive oil for brushing
a packet of filo pastry

Preheat the oven to 200°C/400°F/Gas 6. Drain the spinach in a colander and rigorously press out the water with the back of a wooden spoon. Chop the spinach, still in the colander, with a sharp knife until it is quite fine and leave to cool. Place it on a large plate and season to taste.

Crumble the feta into small cubes and shards and cut the Roquefort into small cubes. Keep the cheeses separate. Place a sheet of filo on your work surface and brush it with olive oil before cutting it into 7.5cm/3in squares, circles, or whatever shape takes your fancy – keep the rest of the filo under a damp cloth as you work. Repeat the process with another two or three sheets of oiled filo.

Place a teaspoon of spinach in the middle of a piece of filo, add a few cubes of cheese, then scrunch the whole into a parcel, leaving a splayed shoot of filo on top. Place on the oiled baking tray, and continue making parcels until you have as many as you want or need. Whack on to the middle shelf of the oven, where they will take between 15–20 minutes to crisp up and goo down. Eat roaring hot off the baking sheet! Or smarten up on plates.

A sweet and simple veggie pie; the kind to keep warm in foil in a knapsack or just to be eaten cold in the hand as a change from common or garden cheese sandwiches. Just make sure you use a really mature Cheddar with character, vibrancy and depth of flavour. A hunk of Montgomery or Quicke's, say. This pie is infinitely more delicious than its ingredients would suggest.

Cheddar Cheese and Onion Pie

SERVES 6

285g/10oz good, strong
  Cheddar, coarsely grated
30g/1oz unsalted butter
1 large onion, peeled and
  chopped finely
110g/4oz potatoes, peeled,
  steamed and diced
2 large eggs
4 tbsp double cream
a sprig of thyme or a bunch of
  flat-leaf parsley, chopped
pinch of cayenne pepper
sea salt and black pepper
shortcrust pastry made with
  340g/12oz flour and 170g/6oz
  unsalted butter (see p.140)
beaten egg for glaze

Preheat the oven to 220°C/425°F/Gas 7. Divide the pastry into two balls, keeping one a little larger than the other. Melt the butter in a pan and gently fry the onion until softened and translucent, then leave to cool. Throw the onions into a bowl with the grated cheese, potato, eggs, cream, thyme or parsley and the seasoning, and mix thoroughly with your fingers.

Roll out the larger ball of pastry and line a shallow greased 23cm/9in tart tin. Tip the cheese and onion mixture into the pastry shell. Moisten the edges of the pastry and cover with the rolled-out top piece, crimping the edges together carefully. Brush beaten egg over the top and bake in the oven for 30 minutes until crisp and golden brown. You can sweat leeks instead of onions, or add buttered apple slices instead of the potato.

This is a musky-breathed pie with a spicy, buttery puff pastry top, but you could just as easily heap the filling into little wholewheat picnic pasties instead, to eat warm or cold. A raita or a Coriander and Mint Chutney served alongside it pits hot and spicy against cool and refreshing.

Vegetable Biriani with a Spiced Pastry Crust

SERVES 6

200g/7oz basmati rice
3 star anise
8 cardamom pods
1 tsp fennel seeds
2 blades of mace
1 tsp cumin seeds
1 tsp turmeric
a handful each of mint, basil and coriander, chopped
6 tbsp yoghurt
2 cloves of garlic
2 green chillies, seeded and thinly sliced
sea salt
1 tbsp panch phora, an Indian spice mix available from spice shops (optional)
1 tbsp ghee or clarified butter
1 cup fresh or frozen peas
1 cup peeled diced pumpkin or squash, roasted until soft
1 cup chopped mushrooms
1 carrot, diced and steamed
a pinch of saffron stamens soaked in a little hot water for 20 minutes
a sheet of puff pastry (see p.141)
beaten egg for glaze
extra fennel seeds to sprinkle on top

Preheat the oven to 190°C/375°F/Gas 5. Half fill a saucepan with water, then add the star anise, cardamom pods, fennel seeds, mace, cumin and turmeric and bring to the boil. Throw in the rice and cook until done, then drain, discarding the pods and mace. Put the herbs, yoghurt, garlic and chillies in a food processor and blend to a paste. Season with salt and set aside.

Heat a large, heavy-bottomed frying pan over a gentle heat, add the panch phora and roast for a minute. Set aside. In the same pan heat the ghee, add the vegetables and fry for a couple of minutes. Take the pan off the heat and add the herb paste, panch phora, rice, saffron and its liquid. Stir them all together, then scrape them into a pie dish. Wet the outside rim of the pie dish with a brush dipped in water and stick a strip of pastry around it. Brush the strip of pastry with beaten egg and place the pie crust on top, pressing them together gently with the tines of a fork. Brush the top with beaten egg and scatter a handful of fennel seeds over the surface. Bake for about 30 minutes, or until the pastry is risen and golden.

Coriander and Mint Chutney

Put a handful each of fresh coriander and mint leaves into the blender with a small chopped onion, a small, seeded, chopped green chilli, the juice of a lemon, sea salt and a couple of tablespoons of red wine vinegar. Process until smooth. Serve with the Vegetable Biriani Pie.

I remember Anna del Conte, the great Italian food writer and historian, saying to me that Italian food and Italian cooking is all about spending your life perfecting two or three traditional dishes. Then you can consider yourself to be a fine cook. In England we have the pie and we have roasting. We are – or can be – exceptionally good at both. So let us get to work on the traditional pies, the ones that have somewhat slipped from grace and pole position, are perceived as difficult, time consuming, a fuss and a fiddle, unmodern. Let us sing their praises and rediscover them. It is not all about raised hot water crusts and suet puddings, though they are the definition of comfort food. These are the sort of pies we should be putting back on the table with a flourish and no apologies. They are our heritage and none the less for it. And they don't need modernist twists to keep their currency, just the finest ingredients you can find and a loving touch in the making.

TRADITIONAL PIES

This is the chicken pie of the traditionals, the apple pie of savouries, the one we all think of first when we think classic pie. Come to it in the late autumn, though not before November, or alight upon it in the lean months of the new year when root vegetables and the cold are waging their culinary war. When the marrow is chilled and the belly best filled with the richly scented, grainy-gravied depths of a steak and kidney pie or pudding. When carbohydrates and red flesh seem like the only answer, the bastion against climate, torpor and the early dark-dayed afternoons, when you can sit and salivate at the prospect of this most handsome and substantial of dishes.

Steak and Kidney Pie

SERVES 6

900g/2lb rump steak, cut into
  bite-sized pieces
450g/1lb ox kidney, cut
  similarly
2 tbsp flour
1 large onion, chopped
85g/3oz butter
570ml/1 pint beef stock, or half
  stock, half red wine
225g/8oz chestnut or
  portobello mushrooms,
  sliced
a bouquet made from
  2 bay leaves and a bunch
  each of fresh thyme,
  rosemary and parsley
sea salt and black pepper
340g/12oz shortcrust or puff
  pastry (see pp.140–141)
beaten egg for glaze

You may cook the filling a day or two in advance if you like, so all you need to do on the day is bake the pie.

Carefully trim the fat and skin from the meat, then toss it and the kidneys in a ziploc bag containing the flour and some salt and pepper. Add two-thirds of the butter to a frying pan and gently sauté the onion, then remove it with a slotted spoon. Add the meat in batches in a single layer, letting it colour briefly on all sides. Transfer the meat to a casserole as you go. Pour the stock, with or without red wine, into the frying pan and bring it to the boil, scraping in any crusty bits from the sides of the pan, then pour it over the meat. Fry the mushrooms in the rest of the butter and add them to the casserole, tucking in the herbs. Cover with a lid and cook in the oven at 150°C/300°F/Gas 2 until the steak and kidney is almost cooked, about 1½ hours. Cool and leave until you want to make the pie.

Preheat the oven to 220°C/425°F/Gas 7. Roll out the pastry and cut off strips to fit around the edges of the pie dish. Brush the rim of the dish with water first so that the strips will adhere. Spoon the filling into the pie dish and cover the whole with a sheet of pastry, pressing the edges together firmly. Decorate with pastry leaves or the like if the mood takes you. Cut a cross in the middle of the pastry through which the steam can escape. Brush the pastry with beaten egg. Bake for 15 minutes, then lower the oven temperature to 170°C/325°F/Gas 3 and cook for a further 45 minutes. Best served with snowy mountains of buttery mashed potato or colcannon, and buttered carrots or cabbage.

This is the ribsticking reminder of times past, but with a thin, crisp crust. There is no need to recreate the slimy grey horrors of claggy, leaden suet that were the province of school dinners. Cooking and cooling the filling in advance is the secret to perfect suet crust. It reduces the steaming time, thus making the pastry crisper and less damply heavy. I think the sealing in of all the meat and its fine juices in the suet coat makes this one of the great winter dishes. When the spoon sinks through the crust and into the spoon-soft meat and its gluey-dark, thickened juices, you smell the scent of heaven on a plate.

Steak and Kidney Pudding

SERVES 6
filling as for the steak and
    kidney pie, cooked and
    cooled (see p.50)

Suet crust:
285g/10oz self-raising flour
110g/4oz beef suet
1 tsp baking powder
sea salt and black pepper
½tsp fresh thyme

Mix all the dry ingredients for the suet crust together in a big bowl, working the suet in well. Stir in some cold water – as little as possible – and work it into a firm dough. Roll the dough out into a large circle on a floured surface and cut away a quarter of it to make a second piece. Butter a 1.5-litre/3-pint pudding basin and slip the larger piece of dough down into it, allowing a little to overhang the rim. Roll out the quarter piece into a circle to form the lid. Spoon the filling into the basin, making sure it comes no higher than 2.5cm/1in below the rim. Brush the overhang with water, then put the lid on and press the edges together, sealing them tightly.

Cover the pudding with a sheet of pleated foil and tie string around it, making a handle at the same time. Lower the basin on to a trivet or some folded foil at the bottom of a pan of boiling water. The water should come two-thirds of the way up the sides of the bowl. Keep at a gentle boil for 1½ hours, checking the water level after an hour. Don't worry if the pudding is left to steam an extra half hour, it will not spoil. Remove the pudding and cut off the string. Take off the foil and serve the pudding piping hot with good English mustard, Brussels sprouts and pommes Anna or mashed potato.

This is an unashamedly and gloriously rich, unctuous dish, a chicken pie flooded with cream and the simple additions of leeks and parsley, not a flavour too far.

Cornish Charter Pie

SERVES 6–8
2 organic chickens, about
   1.4kg/3lb each, jointed
flour
1 large onion, finely chopped
110g/4oz butter
85–110g/3–4oz flat-leaf
   parsley, finely chopped
a fat leek, sliced into slim
   discs
150ml/5fl oz Jersey milk
150ml/5fl oz single cream
290ml/10fl oz double cream
sea salt and black pepper
shortcrust pastry made with
   225g/8oz flour and110g/4oz
   unsalted butter (see p.140)
beaten egg for glaze

Toss the chicken joints in a ziploc bag with a couple of tablespoons of flour and some salt and pepper. Sauté the onion gently in half the butter, then decant it into a large pie dish. Add the rest of the butter to the pan, and when it's hot, sauté the chicken pieces on both sides until they are golden. Put the chicken pieces on top of the onions in a single layer. Simmer the chopped parsley and sliced leek in the milk and single cream for a couple of minutes. Pour all this over the chicken, then add a third of the double cream and season well.

Preheat the oven to 220°C/425°F/Gas 8. Roll out the pastry and cover the pie in the usual way. Cut a couple of crosses in the centre of the pastry to allow the steam to escape and decorate as you wish with the remaining pastry. Brush with beaten egg and bake for 20 minutes. Turn the heat down to 180°C/350°F/Gas 4 and continue to cook for about an hour until the chicken is done. Heat the remaining cream and pour it through a narrow funnel into the cross slit at the centre of the pie. You may serve this hot or allow it to cool, the juices will set to a delectable jelly.

The ultimate crimped parcel, and something well worth making yourself. It really isn't a sweat and home grown is just the best. None of that globby, greasy pastry crust and gristly grey meat lurking under the lid. Here is the classic, but you can experiment with your own combination of textures and flavours. If you can roll out pastry you can make a pasty! And pay attention here. Don't think that this is something to make with butter or any other kind of fat. It ain't. You want the flavour of the lard and the texture it gives to the crust. The point of a pasty is firmness and fullness. It is something to clutch hot between both hands, not something to drip its copious juices down your chin. So, think the great outdoors, picnics, food to eat on the move.

Cornish Pasties

SERVES 4–6

450g/1lb chuck steak
140g/5oz chopped onion
85g/3oz mixed chopped carrot
 and turnip
225g/8oz potato, sliced thin on
 a mandoline
½tsp fresh thyme
sea salt, black pepper
pastry made with 340g/12oz
 flour, 170g/6oz lard, sea salt
 and cold water (see p.140)
beaten egg for glaze

Preheat the oven to 200°C/400°F/Gas 6. Trim the meat of all its gristle and skin, chop it down fine with a heavy, sharp knife, then mix it with your hands into the vegetables and seasoning. Roll out the pastry and cut it into two large circles, dinner-plate size, or 4–6 smaller circles for individual pasties.

Assemble the steak mixture right down the middle of each circle. Brush the pastry rim with beaten egg, then bring the two sides of the pastry up to meet over the top of the filling and pinch them together into a continuous scalloped seam. Pierce two holes on top on either side of the edge through which the steam can escape, and put the pasties on a baking sheet.

Brush them all over with beaten egg and bake for 20 minutes before turning the heat down to 180°C/350°F/Gas 4 for a further 40 minutes. Serve hot, warm or cold.

A beautifully light summer dish of delicate veal, parsley and cream, which you can serve with early summer vegetables – green wands of asparagus, fresh minted peas and tiny violet artichokes.

Parsley Pie

SERVES 6–8
900g/2lb breast of veal, cut
    into 2.5cm/1in cubes
a huge handful of flat-leaf
    parsley, chopped
290ml/10fl oz stock
30g/1oz flour
30g/1oz butter
150ml/5fl oz double cream
sea salt and black pepper
shortcrust pastry made with
    225g/8oz flour and 110g/4oz
    unsalted butter (see p.140)
beaten egg for glaze

Preheat the oven to 180°C/350°F/Gas 4. Put the meat into your pie dish, season it and throw over a green snowstorm of parsley. Add the cold stock and cover with pastry in the usual way. Brush the top with beaten egg and pierce holes in the centre to allow the steam to escape. Bake for 1½ hours. Work the flour and softened butter into a paste and whisk in the cream. Lift the lid of the pie by carefully slitting a corner of the pastry on the join and pour in the cream. Stir it into the stock as much as you can before replacing the lid and returning the pie to the oven for a further 20–30 minutes.

Upper crust, though not in the conventional sense. Crumb rather than crust, but nothing poor man's about this, particularly if you use a good, fruity-strong, aged Cheddar like Montgomery, some oily-scented thyme and a dusky hot hit of cayenne.

Pork Crumble

SERVES 4
675g/1½lb belly pork, boned
55g/2oz seasoned flour
30g/1oz lard or butter
450g/1lb potatoes, peeled and
    sliced
225g/8oz onions, thinly sliced
290ml/10fl oz best dry cider,
    Julian Temperley's Stoke Red
    or Kingston Black is a killer
½ cup brown or white
    breadcrumbs from a stale loaf
½ cup strong Cheddar, grated
cayenne pepper
1 tsp thyme leaves, stripped
    from the stem
sea salt and black pepper

Preheat the oven to 180°C/350°F/Gas 4. Throw the cubed pork into a ziploc bag with the seasoned flour and toss together. Shake off the excess flour and fry the pork on all sides in lard or butter for a few minutes, until lightly golden. Scrape the meat into the dish with the potatoes and onions. Add the hot cider and seasoning, cover and bake in the oven for an hour.

Mix the breadcrumbs, cheese, cayenne and thyme together with your fingers, sprinkle over the surface of the meat and put the dish back in the oven, uncovered. Bake for another 30 minutes, or until the top is gratinéed to a gorgeous golden brown.

It could only be Irish! Swathed in a bog mist of potato, the mutton lurking and seeping its fatty juices underneath, this is a dish for stalwart supporters of the carbohydrate. Those turbo-charged trenchermen and women, who sensibly eschew low fat and lean, consigning it to the unhappy band that believes such food does them good.

Hunter's Pie

SERVES 8

8 generous-sized mutton or
  lamb chops
1 onion, chopped fine
1 carrot, diced small
1 stick of celery, strung and
  finely chopped
some good, dark gravy from
  your Sunday roast, mixed
  with a little stock
1.4kg/3lb potatoes
110g/4oz unsalted butter
150ml/5fl oz milk
salt, black pepper

Put the vegetables in a pan with the gravy and stock and lay the chops on top. Place a layer of greaseproof over the meat and braise until tender and nearly cooked through. Strain the gravy and meat juices, set the chops aside to cool, then skim off the fat from the gravy and set it aside.

Cook the potatoes and drain them in a colander for 5 minutes. Push them through a mouli into a pan and mix with the unsalted butter and milk over a gentle heat. More butter and milk may be necessary and plenty of salt and pepper, please.

Preheat the oven to 180°C/350°F/Gas 4. Butter a large pie dish and line it with two-thirds of the mash. Place the chops on top, cover with the remaining potato, dot with more butter and cook until golden brown. Heat the gravy that you set aside earlier, make a hole in the top of the pie and sloosh in the gravy. Cover the hole up again and serve. Simple.

And before you look away and think 'it's not something I would ever do', at least read these words of cajolery! Let me tell you that buying a hinged mould will be more trouble than pulling and easing the warm paste like a stocking up the insides of a tin, and that this is, truthfully, the easiest kind of pastry you could ever hope to make. And that the simple elegance of the simply accomplished pie will startle you, your children, your guests, but possibly only you will know how easy this apparently complex dish really is. Whether you tell or not depends on how honest you are when people gasp and say how amazing you are, how they could never find the time.

Raised Pies

SERVES 6

Hot water crust:
200g/7oz water
170g/6oz lard
450g/1lb plain flour
½tsp sea salt
1 egg (optional)
beaten egg for glaze

Jellied stock:
bones from the meat used to
  make the filling
2 split pig's trotters or a
  knuckle of veal
2 carrots, chopped
2 stalks of celery, chopped
2 onions, halved but still in
  their skins
a dozen peppercorns
a bouquet of fresh herbs
water to cover

Filling:
Pork
Game
Veal, ham and egg
Mutton and caper
(see pp. 60–62)

To make the crust, bring the water and lard to the boil in a small pan. Tip them into the middle of the flour and salt in a large bowl and swiftly work together with a wooden spoon. You can also do this in a food processor. Add the egg for colour and richness if you like, but it is not essential. Leave the dough until it has cooled to the stage at which you can handle it, but not so long that it is actually cool. Break off a quarter for the lid and put the rest into the base of a hinged pie mould, or a cake tin if you don't have a mould. Push the pastry up the sides with your hands as quickly as you can, sealing any cracks. If the paste collapses as you are working, never fear, it just means it is a little too hot, so squidge it back into a ball, wait and start again. You can shape small pies around jam jars, but you have to be really careful prising the jars out so the pastry stands proud on its own. It is not impossible, I have done it, and manual dexterity isn't my middle name. If you are going to use this method, I would place a strip of brown paper around the pastry and tie string around the circumference so that the pies keep their shape during the cooking. I forgot to do this once and, although it didn't alter the flavour a jot, I ended up with a series of little leaning towers listing heavily to starboard or slouching dangerously to port.

To make the jellied stock, put all the ingredients into a large pan, bring to the boil, skim, then simmer for 3 hours. Strain and boil down the stock until you have about 425ml/15fl oz. It will set to a solid jelly when it cools and is incomparably better than adding gelatine to your stock, but if needs must, go ahead.

The heart of pie country, Melton Mowbray in Leicestershire is home to this most splendiferous of pies. This dish was always shown the bottle of that most old-fashioned of Parson Woodforde condiments, piquant anchovy essence.

Melton Mowbray Pork Pie

SERVES 6

900g/2lb boned shoulder of pork, half minced and half cut into 1cm/½in dice; you need the high fat content of shoulder

225g/8oz thin unsmoked green back bacon, again, half minced, half chopped small (speak sweetly to your butcher)

2–3 tsp fresh sage, finely chopped

½ tsp each cinnamon, nutmeg and allspice; grind the spice yourself, the flavour is so much better

1 tsp anchovy essence

sea salt, black pepper

hot water crust pastry and jellied stock (see p.58)

Put all the meats into a large bowl, add all the seasonings and mix well together by hand. Pack the filling tightly into the pie or pies, then roll out the lid and put it on top with the help of some beaten egg. Cut a central hole, through which the steam can escape, and decorate with pastry trimmings as you will. Brush egg all over the pie and start the cooking at 200°C/400°F/Gas 6 for the first 30 minutes. Reduce the temperature to 170°C/325°F/Gas 3 and cook for a further hour for small pies, or 2 hours for large ones. Cover the top with greaseproof paper if it is darkening too much.

Remove the pie from the oven and take it out of its mould or paper. Brush the sides with beaten egg once more and return to the oven for 10 minutes for a little colour enhancement. Then pour the jellied stock through the hole with a small funnel; the meat will have shrunk considerably. Abandon the pie for at least 24 hours before you tuck in, but longer won't hurt. The beauty of hot water crust pastry is that it absorbs the meat juices and fat on the inside while managing to stay crisp on the outside. Serve with good homemade chutney, a slice of mature Cheddar, a celery salad – I leave it to you.

Veal, Ham and Egg Pie

SERVES 6

675g/1½lb pie veal

340g/12oz piece of unsmoked bacon or uncooked ham

grated zest of a lemon

a handful of flat-leaf parsley, chopped

3 or 4 hard-boiled, shelled eggs

sea salt, black pepper

hot water crust pastry and jellied stock (see p.58)

Dice the veal and the bacon or ham into 1cm/½in cubes, and season with the lemon zest, parsley, sea salt and black pepper. Mix thoroughly, then pack half the mixture into the base of the pastry mould and lay the halved eggs on top. Cover with the rest of the meat mixture and cook and finish as for the Melton Mowbray Pie above.

Richard Guest, the Michelin-starred chef at the lovely Castle Hotel in Taunton, makes stunning individual mutton and caper puddings with the thinnest of suet crusts. Make them, using the suet crust recipe on page 52, in individual tiny pudding basins, but this hot water crust version is utterly droolworthy too. It is not impossible to get mutton these days and the flavour is so much richer and deeper and more developed than lamb, but if you fail to find any, lamb will do.

Mutton and Caper Pies

SERVES 6
1 best end of neck, about
  450g/1lb meat, chopped
  finely, skin removed, a
  quarter of the fat left on
110g/4oz onion, chopped
110g/4oz portobello
  mushrooms, chopped
1 tbsp flat-leaf parsley,
  chopped
½ tbsp tarragon, chopped
1 tbsp capers, drained and
  washed
some gravy from the Sunday
  roast, or from mutton bones
sea salt, black pepper
hot water crust pastry
  (see p.58)

Make individual pie cases with small half-size jam jars. Mix the meat with the onion, mushrooms, herbs, capers and seasoning. Put it into a pan with 120ml/4fl oz of water, bring to the boil and simmer gently for 5 minutes. Cool and then pack into the pastry cups. Bake for 45 minutes. When the pies are ready, pour a little rich brown gravy down through the steam holes. Great hot and great cold.

Game Pie

SERVES 6
450g/1lb game, well-hung
225g/8oz pork back fat, minced
340g/12oz lean pork, minced
225g/8oz lean veal, minced
225g/8oz thin rashers green
  back bacon, 3 of them
  minced (the butcher will do
  this for you if you ask nicely)
a few tbsp Marsala, Madeira
  or dry white wine
grated nutmeg, cinnamon,
  cloves, half a dozen juniper
  berries
a handful of flat-leaf parsley,
  chopped
sea salt, black pepper
hot water crust pastry and
  jellied stock (see p.58)

You can use pheasant, partridge, grouse, woodcock, wild duck, widgeon or any combination for this dish. Remove the game from the bone, cut into small strips, season and set aside. Put the pork, veal and minced bacon in a bowl and splash with the alcohol. Season, add the spices and parsley and mulch it all together with your fingers.

Line the pastry with the rashers and then add layers of game and minced meats, packing them in tight. Proceed as for the Melton Mowbray Pie on page 60. Best eaten cold with cranberry sauce or a tart jelly, ideally crab apple or rowan.

Let's talk turkey. Cold turkey. I'm assuming it's Christmas or Easter in your house, and you've bought only the best, an organic free-range Bronze turkey, not one of the commercial apologies for the real thing. Likewise your ham. Order from Swaddles Farm (01460 234387) who DON'T cure with nitrates, and who will even cook the ham for you if you're overwhelmed by the spirit of Christmas's excesses and sheer hard graft. Whatever. There's always the leftovers, my favourite post-festive indulgence. The worst of the work is over, leaving only the unscheduled surprising of people who turn up at my house in search of sustenance. Expectant, hungry, they deserve dishes that retain the mood but tempt the taste buds.

Turkey and Ham Pie

SERVES 6

450g/1lb cooked turkey meat, light and dark

225g/8oz best ham, cooked on the bone if possible, then pulled into strips

2 carrots, diced small

55g/2oz butter

1 stalk celery, strung and chopped

a dozen or so shallots, peeled and left whole, or the equivalent amount of chopped onion

225g/8oz chestnut or portobello mushrooms, wiped and sliced

30g/1oz flour

425ml/15fl oz milk

2 tsp fresh tarragon or parsley, chopped

sea salt, black pepper

285g/10oz puff pastry (see p.141), or shortcrust if you wish (see p.140)

beaten egg for glaze

Preheat the oven to 200°C/400°F/Gas 6. Cut the turkey meat along the grain into strips and pull the ham into strips of a similar size. Fry the carrots gently in the butter for a few minutes, then add the celery, shallots and mushrooms and continue to cook for about 5 minutes. Scatter in the flour and cook for a minute, then add the hot milk slowly, stirring or whisking constantly to avoid all lumps. Simmer it for a further 5–10 minutes before adding the turkey, ham and seasoning. Remove from the heat, stir everything together well, and add the fresh herbs. Ladle the mixture into your pie dish and allow it to cool. You may do this hours before you need it or the night before if it makes life easier.

Roll out the puff pastry and cover the pie in the usual way, brushing it all over with beaten egg. Bake in the hot oven for 40–60 minutes, or until golden brown and puffed up like an airy pillow.

A squab used to mean a young pigeon – or a short, fat person – but the term seems to have languished, vernacularly speaking. In eighteenth-century Devon, 'squab' lapsed into meaning a lamb or mutton chop. To team lamb with apple may seem unusual when we are so used to the 'à la Normande' way of cooking pork and pheasant, but it works wondrously well, especially with mutton, where it cauterizes the fatty richness. This pie is simple and delicious and to my mind the best way of cooking pigeon, which can be the toughest and driest of any of the game birds.

Squab Pie

SERVES 6–8

4 young squabs (pigeons)
450g/1lb lean mutton or lamb,
   cut into 2.5cm/1in cubes
stock, brown if possible
450g/1lb onions, thinly sliced
900g/2lb Bramley apples,
   peeled, cored and sliced
55g/2oz unrefined caster
   sugar
sea salt and black pepper
340g/12oz shortcrust pastry
   (see p.140)
beaten egg for glaze

Put the cubes of mutton into a pan, cover with stock and simmer very gently for an hour. Remove the meat from the pigeons and cut it into strips.

Preheat the oven to 180°C/350°F/Gas 4. Build the pie filling up in layers, beginning at the bottom with the pigeon meat, then adding the mutton, onions and apples. Pour over 290ml/10fl oz of the strained stock, having removed the top fat, then sprinkle with the sugar and season. Cover with pastry in the usual way and decorate with a pastry apple. Brush with beaten egg and bake for 1½ hours, covering the pastry towards the end if it is beginning to darken too much.

You can, if you want to emulate the old style, scatter a little demerara sugar over the top of the pie half way through the cooking. The Moroccans still do this with their pastillas!

The classic Devonshire squab pie was made with prunes, cinnamon and brown sugar and traditionally topped with clotted cream. I guess it would prove an oddity and talking point to serve one at a dinner party these days, but don't be deterred – it is one of the great pies and deserves a suitable fanfare.

Devonshire Squab Pie

SERVES 6

1 best end of neck of lamb or mutton or 675g/1½lb lamb fillet

900g/2lb sharp eating apples like Cox's orange pippins

16 prunes

2 onions, finely sliced

grated nutmeg, mace and cinnamon

a little dark muscovado sugar

150ml/5fl oz lamb stock

a splash of apple brandy, Kingston Black or Calvados

clotted cream

sea salt and black pepper

shortcrust pastry made with 225g/8oz flour and 55g/2oz each of unsalted butter and lard (see p.140)

Preheat the oven to 200°C/400°F/Gas 6. Slice the meat, peel, core and slice the apples, and chop the unsoaked prunes. Grease a deep pie dish and arrange the meat, apple and onion in layers. Sprinkle the layers cautiously with the mixed spices, seasoning and prunes. Finish with a layer of apples and scatter over an ungenerous 2 teaspoons or so of sugar. Pour the cold stock and brandy over the filling and cover with the pastry in the usual way. Decorate with a pastry apple.

Bake at the above temperature for the first 20–30 minutes. Turn the heat down to 170°C/325°F/Gas 3, cover with greaseproof paper and continue to cook for 45 minutes. Serve hot, hot, hot, with a luscious scoop of clotted cream slipping off the brim.

Breakfast in a pie, brunch, lunch or the perfect picnic. You can add all sorts of early morning ingredients if you feel like a bit of serious substance abuse, carbohydrately speaking: slices of black pudding, cooked slices of Cumberland sausage, mushrooms fried in butter. Go with what you've got and who likes what, but here is the basic model.

Bacon and Egg Pie

SERVES 6

170g/6oz green organic
   streaky bacon, the rind
   snipped off
6 large organic eggs
4–5 tbsp double cream
sea salt, black pepper and
   nutmeg
shortcrust pastry made with
   340g/12oz flour and 170g/6oz
   unsalted butter (see p.140)
beaten egg for glaze

Preheat the oven to 220°C/425°F/Gas 7. Divide the pastry into two balls, the one for the base slightly larger than the one for the top. Line a greased shallow tart tin with the larger piece of pastry.

Cook the bacon in a pan until frazzled and burnished brown and drain thoroughly on kitchen paper. When cool, snip the bacon into the pastry base. Break the eggs into the pie, one at a time, keeping them whole. Pour over the double cream and season with salt, pepper and nutmeg.

Roll out the remaining pastry, moisten the edges of the pie and cover with the top sheet. Press the edges together and decorate as you will with the trimmings before brushing the pastry with the beaten egg. Bake in the middle of the oven for 30 minutes until golden brown. Tomato ketchup or brown sauce on the table, please.

Plagiarizing with permission may seem something of a contradiction in terms, but that is the neatest way to explain this chapter. All good cooks steal – and beg and borrow – the word magpie was invented for us. And even the more original of us, if there is such a breed, are not averse to 'anthologizing' each other's recipes, tweaking, reworking and reinventing them. I had a similar chapter with recipes from some of my favourite cooks in *The Art of the Tart*, so there seemed every good reason to do it again here – and not just with the professionals. Some of my friends are exceptionally good home cooks, and I would as soon go to dinner with them as I would to the best restaurant. Good home cooking is not inferior, merely a different experience – and in the hands of these chosen few, a pretty hot experience at that. I have steered my chosen few to come up with savoury or sweet pies that best show what they like to cook and the way they like to cook it. These dishes give you a taste of their very different, and often eclectic, styles.

OTHER PEOPLE'S PIES

My first introduction to Michel was when my editor, Susan Haynes, informed me that he would be one of the guests at the publisher's dinner I was cooking the next day. No pressure then! Michel, two-Michelin-starred chef of Le Gavroche, also happens to be one of the most generous and least egocentric of his profession. If you ask him for a recipe he scurries off mid-service to write it down, and yes, his chocolate brownie recipe is the richest and best in the world. The two most recent meals I've had at Le Gavroche have been two of the most faultlessly delicious – and fun – I can remember, and it is a place I would always return to, knowing that it offers a timeless sense of occasion and unshowy opulence in a way that so few restaurants do nowadays, in this age of cloning and copying. Here is a simply delicious, deliciously elegant, classic French tourte.

Michel Roux's Tourte au Jambon et Tomme de Pyrénées

SERVES 8
675g/1½lb best quality ham, thinly sliced
170g/6oz hard ewe's milk cheese from the Pyrenees, coarsely grated
béchamel sauce, made with 200ml/7fl oz full-fat milk, 30g/1oz each of butter and flour, salt, pepper, nutmeg
600g/1lb 5oz puff pastry (see p.141)
beaten egg for glaze

Madeira truffle vinaigrette:
100ml/3½fl oz Madeira reduced to 3 tbsp
55g/2oz black truffles, chopped
2 tbsp truffle juice
2 tbsp Xeres vinegar
1 tbsp white truffle oil
1 tbsp olive oil
salt, black pepper

For the béchamel, bring the milk to the boil and in a separate pan make a roux with the butter and flour. Whisk the milk into this and boil, whisking continuously. Season with salt, pepper and grated nutmeg, loosely cover and leave to cool.

Roll out the puff pastry into two 23cm/9in circles. Layer the ham, cheese and béchamel on one of the circles, leaving a rim of 4cm/1½in around the outside. The top layer should be ham, pressed well down to form an even dome. Brush the pastry rim with egg and cover with the other piece of puff pastry. Press well to seal the edges and cut a neat, wave-shaped rim. Refrigerate for 2 hours. Brush with egg and use the point of a sharp knife to decorate the top with swirling lines like a Pithiviers.

Preheat the oven to 190°C/375°F/Gas 5. Cook for 30 minutes or until puffed up and golden. Leave to rest for 20 minutes before cutting. Serve with a little salad and, if feeling extravagant, a Madeira truffle vinaigrette. For the vinaigrette, simply mix all the ingredients together and chill.

Richard Corrigan's food is adjective defying, and his is one of the handful of restaurants I would rather eat in above all others. One of the most talented and original – in the best sense of the word, not because he is always trying to reinvent the wheel – of chefs I know, he has ploughed his own furrow, sowed his own style and earned the accolade he deserves, without being hung up on the theatricality of the circus that the whole restaurant business has turned into. He served a more complicated version of this dish at my launch dinner for *Good Tempered Food*, so if you don't want to cook this, book a table at Lindsay House, Romilly Street in Soho, in the game season, and get him to cook it for you. You can substitute partridge or pheasant for the grouse.

Richard Corrigan's Grouse en Croute

SERVES 2
1 old grouse, breasts removed
unsalted butter
2 Savoy cabbage leaves
duxelle of mushrooms made
   with 110g/4oz mushrooms
   very finely chopped, a tiny bit
   of minced garlic and a
   couple of finely minced
   shallots, all cooked in butter
   or, better still, duck fat, until
   softened
285g/10oz puff pastry
   (see p.141)
beaten egg for glaze

Sauce:
grouse carcass broken up
2 carrots
1 leek
a clove of garlic
walnut-sized piece of butter
150ml/5fl oz red wine or
   Madeira
150ml/5fl oz chicken stock

To make the sauce, roast the grouse bones lightly – don't let them over-colour. Remove the bones and add a mirepoix of the finely diced vegetables to the grouse fat in the roasting tin, then roast them until golden brown. Deglaze on top of the stove with red wine, scraping all the bits in well, then reduce by half, letting the red wine bubble away merrily. Add the chicken stock and reduce that by half too. Strain the sauce through a fine sieve and set aside.

Preheat the oven to 200°C/400°F/Gas 6. Seal the grouse breasts lightly and quickly in butter, before laying each one on a Savoy cabbage leaf which you've blanched in boiling water for 30 seconds. Spoon a tablespoon of the duxelle over each breast and spread it evenly over the meat. Wrap into parcels, then roll out two circles of pastry, and wrap each parcel in pastry, sealing the edges with beaten egg. Bake in the oven for 15 minutes until risen and golden. Richard only cooks his for 9 minutes at Lindsay House and they emerge perfectly pink and bloody, not raw, but his is a roaring industrial oven. Leave for 4 minutes before serving. Reheat the sauce, adding little bits of butter to enrich it, and serve separately. Richard serves this dish with Brussels sprouts tossed in butter with crisp lardons and sliced chestnuts.

I love Nigel's food, I love Nigel's writing. That's all there is to it really, so there is no point in my describing his delectable creation, when he sent the lyrical accompaniment below with this delicious recipe. If anyone can seduce you with words into cooking anything, Nigel is your man.

'This is a sort of frying-pan pie (I do it in black cast iron). The crust, both top and bottom, is made of mashed potato, the top made crispy with a layer of Parmesan. The filling is very softly cooked onions and Stilton, though I'm sure Gorgonzola or Cashel Blue would be just as good. You won't get a decent slice out of it, it tends to come in more of a slouching mass, scooped straight from the pan. Look, I don't eat this sort of thing every day. Sometimes you just need comfort food of the highest order. The peeling of the potatoes and slow cooking of the onions takes a good hour, so it's not something to throw together for a mid-week supper. It is what I call weekend food. The slow cooking of the onions is essential so they turn soft and sweet and melt with the cheese. Expect this to take a good 20–25 minutes over a low heat. All this molten cheese and mashed potato needs something contrasting. I usually serve lots of vivid green spinach or frills of kale. Either way they need no butter.'

Nigel Slater's Stilton, Onion and Potato 'Frying-Pan' Pie

SERVES 6
1.5kg/3¼lb floury potatoes
4 medium onions
85g/3oz butter
225g/8oz Stilton
150ml/5fl oz milk
30g/1oz Parmesan, grated

Put a large pan of water on to boil. Peel the potatoes and cut them into halves or quarters, then add them to the boiling water. When it comes back to the boil, add a little salt and turn down to a lively simmer. Check the potatoes now and again; they should be tender in 15 minutes or so.

While the potatoes cook, peel the onions, cut them in half, then cut each into five or six segments. Put them into a heavy-based frying pan with 40g/1 oz of the butter and let them cook over a moderate to low heat, stirring from time to time. They will need 20–25 minutes to become thoroughly soft and sticky.

Bring the milk to the boil and turn off the heat. Drain the potatoes and tip them into the bowl of a food mixer fitted with a beater attachment. Mix slowly adding the milk and remaining butter. Beat to a smooth mash, stopping well before it becomes gluey.

Preheat the oven to 200°C/400°F/Gas 6. Butter the base and sides of a heavy 28cm/11in frying pan with a metal handle or a similar diameter baking dish – I use a black cast-iron frying pan – then spoon in a half of the mashed potato. Smooth the potato a little, then add the onions and a grinding of black pepper. Crumble the Stilton over the onions. Pile the rest of the mashed potato over the top and smooth lightly with the back of the spoon or rubber spatula.

Dust over the grated Parmesan then bake in the preheated oven for 25–30 minutes, by which time the top will be pale gold and the filling will be bubbling up around the edges.

This is a fabulous Moroccan pie from Claudia Roden's lovely book *Tamarind and Saffron*, which she describes as 'light and tasty and makes a grand party dish'. Claudia is a legend, simply one of the most accomplished food writers, historians, ethnographers of her generation, whose *The Book of Jewish Food* and *A Book of Middle Eastern Food* will be the benchmark for us all for generations to come.

Claudia Roden's Chicken and Onion Filo Pies

SERVES 8

4 organic chicken breast fillets, skinned and boned

5 large onions

4 tbsp sunflower oil

½–¾ tsp ground ginger

1½ tsp ground cinnamon, plus more to sprinkle at the end

salt

juice of half a lemon

a large bunch of coriander (about 110g/4oz weight with stems), finely chopped

8 sheets filo pastry

4–5 tbsp melted butter or oil

1 egg yolk for glaze

icing sugar (optional)

Chop the onions in batches in the food processor. Put them into a large saucepan with the oil, ginger, cinnamon, a little salt and lemon juice and the chicken fillets. Put the lid on and cook on a low heat for about 15 minutes. Take out the chicken pieces and continue cooking the onions without the lid on so that the liquid evaporates. Cook until the onions have been reduced to a creamy sauce and you can see the oil sizzling – it takes about an hour – stirring every so often.

Cut the chicken into smallish pieces and put them back into the pan with the onion sauce. Add the coriander and mix very well. Taste and add salt and more of the flavourings if necessary. Preheat the oven to 180°C/350°F/Gas 4.

Open out the sheets of filo when you are ready to use them and be ready to work fast as they dry out. Leave them in a pile and brush the top one with melted butter or oil. Take about one-eighth of the chicken and onion mixture and put it in a flat mound on the sheet about 7.5cm/3in from one edge, in the middle. Fold the edge over the filling, and turn the packet over with the filling, folding the side ends of the sheet up at different turns so as to end up with a flat parcel with several layers of pastry on either side.

Continue with the rest of the filo sheets and filling, and place all the parcels on a sheet of foil on a baking tray. Brush the tops with the egg yolk mixed with 1 tsp of water. Bake for 35–40 minutes, until crisp and golden.

Serve hot. Pass round little pots of icing sugar and cinnamon for everyone to sprinkle on if they wish.

Filo pastry is the most common of the many doughs used in the Middle East to make pies. Claudia says that meat pies are traditionally made in little triangular shapes and that the classic Arab filling here is called 'tatbila'.

Claudia Roden's Filo Triangles with Minced Meat, Onions and Pine Nuts

MAKES ABOUT 20

225g/8oz minced lamb or beef
1 small onion, chopped
2 tbsp sunflower oil
¾ tsp ground cinnamon
¼ tsp ground allspice
2 tbsp pine nuts, lightly
  toasted
5 or 6 sheets of filo pastry
3 tbsp melted butter or oil
salt , black pepper

For the filling, fry the onion in the oil until golden. Add the meat and fry lightly, crushing it with a fork and turning it over until it changes colour. Add salt, pepper, cinnamon and allspice. Stir in the pine nuts.

Preheat the oven to 180°C/350°F/Gas 4. Take out the sheets of filo only when you are ready to use them, since they quickly dry out. Cut the sheets into four rectangles, measuring about 30 x 12.5cm/ 12 x 5in), and put them in a pile on top of each other. Brush the top strip lightly with melted butter or oil.

Take a heaped teaspoon of filling. Place it at one end of the strip of filo, about 3cm/1¼in from the edge. Fold the end over the filling. Now pick up a corner and fold diagonally, making a triangle. Continue to fold until the whole strip has been turned into a triangular packet, making sure that you close any holes as you fold so that the filling does not ooze out. If the filo sheets are too thin and look likely to tear, use two strips together and brush with melted butter or oil between.

Place the little packets close to each other on a greased baking tray and brush the tops with oil or melted butter. Bake for 30 minutes or until crisp and golden.

Meat loaf is one of those things that even clueless-in-the-kitchen can cook. It is cooking by numbers, but nothing wrong with that – small triumphs fuel ambition in the kitchen! Here you can blag further by buying the puff pastry, thus presenting a dish that looks as though it were actually made by a competent, nay keen, cook. And it is foolproof, child's play. You could get your child to do it for you. It's only about stirring ingredients together and rolling out a sheet of dough. And the fresh tomato sauce that is great with it, my daughter Miranda first made when she was nine, so we're not talking postgrad here. This pie is the culinary equivalent of a starter home.

Deborah's Luxury Meat Loaf Pie

SERVES 8

450g/1lb best beef mince

225g/8oz good organic pork sausage meat

55g/2oz fresh breadcrumbs, white or brown

1 large onion, finely minced

1 large egg

2 cloves garlic, finely chopped

2 tbsp fresh parsley, chopped

1 tbsp fresh thyme, chopped

1 dsrtsp tomato purée

Lea and Perrins Worcestershire sauce

sea salt, black pepper

12 quails' eggs, hard boiled and shelled

450g/1lb puff pastry (bought or see p.141)

beaten egg for glaze

Preheat the oven to 190°C/375°F/Gas 5. Put the mince, sausage meat and breadcrumbs into a large bowl. Add all the other ingredients except the quails' eggs, and gunge them around with your hands to mix thoroughly. Press half the mixture into a loaf tin that you have lightly brushed with olive oil. Lay the quails' eggs along the centre of the mixture, pressing them down gently. Cover with the rest of the mixture, put the tin in the oven and cook for 1¼ hours. Remove the meat loaf from the oven and cool completely.

Reset the oven to 220°C/425°F/Gas 7. Roll out the puff pastry. Remove the meat loaf from the tin and wrap it completely in pastry, sealing the edges with beaten egg. Bake for 35–40 minutes until golden and beautifully risen.

If you want to serve this hot, make a spicy tomato sauce to go with it. It's also excellent cold picnic food, needing no more than a good lettuce and some homemade mayonnaise.

Passed down from Dom Lane's great-grandmother, Amy Butler, to his paternal grandmother, Elsie Lane and hence to Dom, who describes it thus: 'The recipe is anecdotal and varies from household to household, but is traditional across Lancashire in one form or another. My grandmother tells me that the recipe gained popularity among women who worked in the mills. They could put the casserole element of the pie in the oven when they left the house first thing and a neighbour would pop in the back-door mid-morning and replace the pot lid with the suet crust so that it was ready on her return at lunch-time.

A cheap and hearty meal, my grandmother cooked this pie at least a couple of times a week in the winters before the war. She says she pined for it while she was in the WRAF and looked forward to it when she was home on leave. I have fond memories of visits to grandma's when I was young and this was always my favourite supper.'

Lancashire Potato Pie

SERVES 4
450g/1lb braising or stewing steak, cut into cubes and fat trimmed off
225g/8oz ox liver, finely chopped
4 small onions, finely chopped
4 medium potatoes
stock or water
suet crust pastry (see p.52)
salt, black pepper

Place the trimmed chunks of steak in a large, lidded casserole. Add '2 penn'orth' of ox liver – about 55g/2oz – per person, which ensures a lovely gravy. Add the chopped onions and the potatoes, cut into chunks the same size as the meat. Season with salt and pepper and stir together. Add stock or water, just enough to moisten and aid the cooking. Put the lid on and cook in a medium oven for a couple of hours. The desired effect is 'mushy' as Mrs Lane describes it. Once the filling has attained this state of mushiness, the meat and potato having combined with the natural juices to create a wonderfully wholesome singularity, remove the casserole lid and replace with a thick layer of suet crust pastry. Turn the oven up to 200°C/400°F/Gas 6 and cook until golden brown.

This pie is truly delicious with all the necessary characteristics of solid English working-class fare, stodgy but honest, filling, nutritious. Traditionally served with pickled red cabbage and a glass of stout.

I have had many a good dinner and lunch in Bristol's best restaurant, Markwicks, with the proprietors Stephen and Judy Markwick. Stephen is one of the most talented chefs I know, whose reputation, had he cheffed in London, would have been altogether more legendary. He has finally hung up his ladles after 25 years of 80 or 90 hours a week slog, but insists he has not permanently left the stove. Meanwhile try the pie.

Stephen Markwick's Chicken and Mushroom Pie

SERVES 6–8
1 roasted chicken, cold
55g/2oz butter
55g/2oz flour
570ml/1 pint good chicken
   stock
1 tsp Dijon mustard
lemon juice
1 onion, finely chopped
225g/8oz mushrooms
a good splosh of white wine
a handful each of tarragon and
   parsley, chopped
sea salt and black pepper
shortcrust or puff pastry
   (see p.141)
beaten egg for glaze

Make a roux-based sauce in the usual way with the butter, flour and chicken stock and season well. Add the mustard and a spritz of lemon juice. Sweat the chopped onion and sliced mushrooms together in a little butter, add the splosh of white wine and decant the whole lot into the sauce, stirring it over a gentle heat for a few minutes.

Strip the chicken flesh from the carcass, removing all the skin and fat as you go, and tear it into good-sized pieces for the pie. Add the chicken and chopped herbs to the sauce with the fresh herbs and check the seasoning. Set aside to cool.

Preheat the oven to 200°C/400°F/Gas 6. Pile the chicken mixture into a pie dish and top with the pastry lid. Brush with egg in the usual way and bake for about 30 minutes or until bubbling and golden brown. Serve with mash and a green veg or salad.

Sally is Somerset's answer to Alice Waters. At her new café, she serves simple, but elegant and perfectly executed food made from the sort of ingredients that are totally above and beyond suspicion. She sources from the best growers, suppliers, fishmongers and rearers, and everything from the breads to the cakes – and baking is her real forte – are as good as you'd find in a more serious and pretentious restaurant. When she opened her new café in Bath Place, Taunton at the beginning of the year, those of us who'd used her as our Saturday lunch canteen in her previous incarnation, breathed a collective sigh of relief. We'd suffered withdrawal symptoms for months while she found and then equipped the new venue. Here is her light version of a fish pie that she 'pinched from an Italian restaurant in Soho', and which I somehow had to guess at from the minimalist instructions! I made mine with Forman's wild smoked salmon, which Sally didn't frown upon when I told her. Potatoes cut the oily-fished richness most successfully.

Sally Edwards' Hot-Roast Salmon, Leek and Potato Tourte

SERVES 6

225g/8oz hot-roast salmon

450g/1lb potatoes, cooked and skinned

450g/1lb leeks, thinly sliced

butter

2 eggs

2 heaped tbsp double cream

1 heaped tbsp mascarpone

chopped herbs, such as dill, chervil and parsley, as you wish

sea salt, black pepper

a packet of filo pastry

Slice the cooked potatoes and leave them to cool. Sauté the leeks in butter, season and leave to cool.

Preheat the oven to 200°C/400°F/Gas 6. Brush a Swiss roll tin with melted butter, line with a layer of filo and brush that with melted butter. Cover the filo with sliced potatoes, followed by a layer of cold, cooked leeks, then the hot-roast salmon. Pour over a mixture of the eggs, cream and mascarpone, all whisked together and seasoned well. Sprinkle over the chopped herbs.

Brush another couple of sheets of filo with melted butter, place them on top and trim the edges. Bake for 20–25 minutes until browned and just set. Leave to rest for a few minutes before serving.

My mother makes a mean fish pie, decked with prawns, hard-boiled eggs and parsley, the kind of dish one yearns for after being away from home for too long and suffering from a surfeit of hotels, restaurants or plain bad cooking. This is old-fashioned comfort food. I always loved it, my brother Daniel detested it.

Mama's Fish Pie

SERVES 6

400g/13oz fresh haddock
400g/13oz natural smoked
  haddock
285g/10oz or so large prawns
290ml/10fl oz full-cream milk
30g/1oz butter
40g/1½oz flour
juice of half a lemon
anchovy essence (optional)
6 hard-boiled eggs
a generous handful of flat-leaf
  parsley, chopped
sea salt, black pepper
mash made with 900g/2lb
  potatoes, butter and milk

Put the fish in an ovenproof dish large enough to contain it in one layer, then pour over the milk and about 290ml/10fl oz of water. Cover with foil and bake for about 15 minutes or until the fish flakes away easily from the skin and bones. Meanwhile, make your mashed potato with lots of butter and hot milk and season well.

Preheat the oven to 190°C/375°F/Gas 5. Make a roux with the butter and flour and stir in enough of the fish poaching liquid to make a sauce the consistency of double cream. Season to taste, adding lemon juice and anchovy essence if you like it. Fold in the flaked fish, prawns, sliced hard-boiled eggs and parsley and put into a pie dish deep enough to hold the potato topping. Make furrows in the potato with the tines of a fork and dot with butter. Bake for about 30 minutes, or until the potato is lightly browned.

Chef proprietor of Le Quartier Vert in Bristol, a fine restaurant with its own bustling, relaxed style, Barney has a watchful and uncompromising eye for the best ingredients. This is what he wrote of his pie:

'Twenty years ago, student, summer holiday working in a restaurant on the Ille d'Aix, Le Pressoir – still there 30 years on – and staying with my French girlfriend in Royan. This is her mother's fish pie. I wish I could remember Annie's mother's name. Her father – who worked at the railway station – was called Albert. I remember him, because for pudding he made me eat 6 cloves of barely crushed garlic with an old goat's cheese to pass the manliness test. Annie's mother made the best omelette in the world, but her fish pie was even better. I have substituted her sublimely light pastry crust for one with potato in it, because I'm no good at pastry but even I can manage this one. The important and brilliant thing about this pie is that the bouillon used for

750g/1lb 10oz firm white fish,
filleted and boned (use
coley, halibut, monkfish,
conger eel or sole, but not
cod, haddock or hake)
140g/5oz large crevettes roses
(Mediterranean prawns),
peeled
500g/1lb 2oz mussels or clams
or a combination

Court bouillon:
200ml/7fl oz dry white wine
200ml/7fl oz water
½ onion, coarsely chopped
2 bay leaves and a sprig of
thyme
a few white peppercorns
1 lemon wedge

Sauce base:
10g/½oz butter
50g/scant 2 oz flour
2 tsp Dijon mustard
150ml/5fl oz double cream
salt and pepper

Vegetables:
knob of unsalted butter
1 small white onion, finely
diced
1 carrot, finely diced
½ stick celery, finely diced
½ bulb fennel, finely diced
½ leek, finely diced
1 clove garlic finely minced
a handful of parsley, chopped

Potato pastry crust:
285g/10oz cooked potato,
grated
285g/10oz flour
½ tsp bicarbonate of soda
1 tsp salt
black pepper
200g/7oz unsalted butter
1 egg beaten with a splash of
milk for glaze

poaching the fish and mussels becomes part of the sauce. You need super-fresh fish (it's not a cheap dish anyway) and good parsley. And if the wine you are drinking with the pie is not too expensive, use a couple of glasses of that for the bouillon.

Barney Haughton's 'Annie's Mother's' Seafood Pie

To make the pastry, mix the flour, bicarb, salt and pepper together in a bowl. Rub in the butter, looking for that light, crumbly texture. With a knife, chop in the grated potato until well mixed and slightly doughy. Add just enough cold water to get the mixture to form a compact but not solid ball. Cover and refrigerate.

For the court bouillon, put all the ingredients into a shallow pan and simmer for 10 minutes. Working in three batches so that the temperature of the bouillon doesn't drop too much, poach the fish until only just cooked, 10–15 seconds per batch. Remove the fish from the bouillon and set aside. Cook the mussels until they open and leave to cool before removing them from the shell and adding to the fish. Chuck the coarsely chopped prawns in with the fish. Strain the bouillon through a fine sieve, you should have about 500ml/18fl oz. Reduce it over a gentle heat to about 340ml/12fl oz.

Make the béchamel by adding the cream slowly to the butter and flour roux until thick, then adding the mustard and plenty of seasoning. Now add the bouillon. You should end up with a deliciously creamy, fishy velouté.

Next prepare the vegetables. Put a knob of butter into a large pan and heat gently. Add onion and cook for 3–6 minutes, then add the carrots, celery, fennel and leeks, cooking for a further 3–6 minutes. Finally add the garlic for another 3–4 minutes. Add a couple of splashes of water, cover and simmer until the vegetables are soft and opaque. Mix in the parsley.

Preheat the oven to 190°C/375°F/Gas 5 and assemble the dish. Mix the sauce and vegetables together, check for seasoning. Put the fish, mussels and prawns in a 1.5-litre/3-pint pie dish and pour over the warm sauce and the vegetable mixture. Roll out the pastry – not too thin, this is a thick potato crust. Place the pastry carefully over the pie, cutting a steam hole in the middle, and brush with the beaten egg and milk glaze. Bake for 30–40 minutes.

This is the fourth book of mine that my friend George has contributed to, and I have to say my cooking life would be the poorer without her. She manages to combine an encyclopaedic knowledge of all things epicurean with fun, relish and greed on the one hand, and adherence to the highest standards and expectations on the other. And we do just work in the kitchen, an idea of mine or hers triggering a new dish, the revision of an old one, or the inspiration for something completely different. And who said two bossy cooks in the kitchen is two too many? In our case it works. Halves the work and doubles the pleasure actually. Here's the bare bones of an idea she sent, with my additions lest the shorthand should fall short recipe-wise.

George Morley's Plum and Almond Pie

SERVES 6–8

1kg/2¼lb plums, halved and stoned
1 tbsp muscovado sugar, or to taste
1 tsp cinnamon
1 tsp cornflour
1 packet whole blanched almonds
a sheet of puff pastry (see p.141)
caster sugar
milk

Sprinkle the muscovado sugar, cinnamon and cornflour over the plums in a bowl, toss gently, then leave long enough for the juices to begin to run. Spread the almonds on a baking tray and toast them briefly in the oven – until they begin to scent the room is the best test, they over-brown fiendishly quickly. Chop them coarsely, with a mezza luna if you have one.

Preheat the oven to 200°C/400°F/Gas 6. Throw everything into a pie dish. Top with pastry in the usual way, brush the surface with milk and scatter some unrefined caster sugar, a handful should do it, over the top. Bake for 10 minutes, then turn the temperature down to 180°C/350°F/Gas 4 and continue to cook for another 30 minutes or so, until beautifully golden on top. At it's best, George says, half an hour after it has come out of the oven, with cream or proper custard.

Sally Clarke's Quince, Apple, Prune, Almond and Orange Polenta Pie

SERVES 8

zest and juice of 3 oranges
juice of 2 lemons
1 cinnamon stick
140g/5oz sugar
1 glass sweet white wine
  (optional)
3 large quinces, peeled, cored
  and quartered
3 large Braeburn (or similar)
  apples, peeled, cored and
  quartered
16 pre-soaked prunes,
  quartered
1 tsp ground cinnamon
2 tbsp demerara sugar plus a
  little for sprinkling
85g/3oz whole almonds,
  blanched in boiling water
  and peeled

Pastry:

100g/3½oz ground polenta
255g/9oz white flour
170g/6oz butter
170g/6oz sugar
3 egg yolks
1 egg
good pinch of salt
beaten egg for glaze

Place the citrus juices in a stainless steel pan with the cinnamon stick, sugar and wine if using. Add the prepared quince quarters. Barely cover with cold water, cover with a tight-fitting lid and bring to a simmer. Continue to cook very gently until the fruit is tender. Remove the quince with a slotted spoon, cool and slice each piece in half lengthways. Reduce the fruit juices over a high heat until syrupy, then leave to cool.

Meanwhile make the pastry. Place the polenta and white flour in a bowl with the chilled butter and rub in until it resembles rough breadcrumbs. Add the sugar and salt and mix well. Mix the egg yolks and whole egg together, then gradually mix in the flour until it binds together. Gently knead the dough until it is almost smooth. Divide into two balls, wrap and chill for at least an hour before rolling out.

Preheat the oven to 170°C/325°F/Gas 3. Roll the balls of pastry out to about 30cm/12in, one slightly smaller than the other. Line a 20–25cm/8–10in loose-based, fluted tart tin with the larger disc and leave to chill again for 20 minutes. Bake blind (see p.140) for about 20 minutes or until almost crisp. Leave the other disc of pastry covered in the fridge.

Slice the apples thinly and toss in a bowl with the orange zest, ground cinnamon and demerara sugar. Place half the apples in the pastry case, add the quince pieces, almonds and prunes in an even layer on top, then cover with the remaining apples. Cover with the other disc of pastry, sealing the edges with water and crimping them together. Brush with beaten egg, sprinkle with demerara sugar and bake for 40 minutes until the pastry is crisp and golden and the fruit feels tender when pierced with a skewer. Allow the pie to cool a little, remove from the tin and serve with the quince syrup and some whipped cream or crème fraîche.

Cooks don't come better than Simon, and I always love his no-nonsense, dictatorial tone that no half-way decent cook would dare to stray from for a milli-second. Simon remembers this as THE comfort recipe of his childhood, which his mother 'would always have ready waiting, warm and weeping pink juice, on the back of the Aga for my first night home from boarding school at the beginning of the summer holidays. If you are able to buy slightly over-ripe strawberries for this, then do. They can often be a bargain price and work just as well as prime specimens.'

Simon Hopkinson's Strawberry Pie

SERVES 6
1kg/2¼lb strawberries, hulled
   and cut in half lengthways
75g/2½oz caster sugar
a little butter
1 beaten egg mixed with
   1 tbsp milk

Pastry:
225g/8oz chilled butter, cut
   into small pieces
500g/1lb 2oz self-raising flour
a pinch of salt
3 tbsp ice-cold water
1 egg yolk

In a food processor, electric mixer or manually, blend together the butter, flour and salt until it resembles fine breadcrumbs. Now tip into a large bowl and gently mix in the water and egg yolk with cool hands or a knife, until amalgamated. Put into a plastic bag and chill in the fridge for at least an hour before rolling.

Preheat the oven to 200°C/400°F/Gas 6. Lightly grease a loose-bottomed cake tin, 20 x 4cm/8 x 1½in, with butter. Roll out two-thirds of the pastry into a circle; don't make it too thin. Carefully line the tin with this, allowing a slight excess to flop over the rim. Tip in the strawberries, sprinkle over 55g/2oz of the sugar and shake the tin slightly so that the sugar disperses. Lightly press down with your hands. Now brush a little of the beaten egg and milk around the edge of the pastry that lies just above the rim of the cake tin. Roll out the remaining third of pastry slightly thinner than the base. Carefully lift on to the pie and lightly press the two pastry edges together. With a sharp knife, cut through the joined edges almost flush up to the rim. With your fingers, knock the edges together to form a crinkled edge all the way around. Brush the whole surface with beaten egg and milk and sprinkle with the rest of the caster sugar. Make a couple of incisions in the centre of the pastry lid to allow steam to escape.

Put into the oven on the middle shelf with an empty roasting tin underneath. The reason for the tin is to catch any dribbles that almost certainly will ooze out of the pie as it cooks. These juices may burn a little so watch out. Cook for about 15 minutes at this temperature and then turn down to 170°C/325°F/Gas 3 for a further 30–40 minutes until the pastry is a rich golden colour. Leave in the tin until lukewarm, before removing and placing on a large round plate. Cut into wedges and serve with clotted or whipped cream.

A chance letter, accompanied by her delightful volume of poems, *The Watercourse*, arrived via my publishers this summer from Cynthia Zarin in New York, who wrote having read and enjoyed my first book, *West of Ireland Summers, A Cookbook*. And so began an e-mail correspondence based on food and literature. Since it became clear early in our correspondence that Cynthia is a passionately keen and well-informed cook, I asked her to be a contributor. Here is her piece of pie:

'The recipe is from an Austrian cook that Alice B. Toklas calls Frederich. Here's a little about him from her. "He would make us ice cream in individual moulds in the form of eggs on a nest of coloured spun sugar. He delighted in making cakes that represented objects appropriate to each person, a book for Gertrude Stein, a rose for Sir Francis Rose, a peacock for a very vain young lady and a little dog for me....And he told us that he and Hitler had been born in the same village and that anyone in the village was like all the others and that they were all a little strange. This was in 1936 and we already knew Hitler was very strange...." Here is Alice B. Toklas via Frederich via me; the main difference is walnuts vs almonds.'

Cynthia Zarin's Linzer Torte

SERVES 6
1 pot raspberry jam
1 cup flour
½ cup unsalted butter
½ cup walnuts
½ sugar
yolks of 2 hard-boiled eggs
cinnamon
grated nutmeg
grated zest of a small lemon
3 tsp dark rum
beaten egg for glaze

Quickly combine the flour and very cold unsalted butter using your fingers. In the following order add the walnuts, which you've ground up in a spice grinder (take care not to process to a paste), sugar, the egg yolks put through a sieve, cinnamon, nutmeg and lemon zest. Add three teaspoons of dark rum. Refrigerate in clingfilm in a ball for a few hours, then roll out three-quarters of the dough.

Preheat the oven to 180°C/350°F/Gas 4. Fit the dough into a buttered flan ring and fill with raspberry jam (I use Hero but it doesn't matter what brand as long as it's very jammy). If you're good with your hands, use up the rest of the dough by making strips of lattice across the top. Otherwise decorate the top with abandon, using little pieces of dough you've rolled up into ropes and swags. I like to make a tree, with a little crescent moon in the corner. If you do this be sure to leave enough room between the branches so that when the torte cooks, the branches don't melt into one another. Brush with beaten egg and bake for about 30 minutes. The main thing you're after here is the delicious crust. The jam is simply a foil.

A is for apple pie. The nursery rhyme lives with us from our earliest years and culinary memories. As does the scent of autumn apples steaming in a pie; pouring hot, silky, vanilla-flecked custard over thick gluey-appled pastry triangles; pushing a clot of thick yellow cream on to the sugared pastry top with your fingers; or dropping a cold scoop of the best homemade vanilla ice cream over the summit, the hot beating the cold into melting submission. Apple pie is the alpha and omega of pies – well, at least of sweet pies – and there are, I'm sure, as many versions as there are cooks, but that is the joy of it. From cheese crusts and spices to crumble tops and gooky molasses-sugared tops punctuated with scrunched walnuts; from the plainest pie to the traditional winter welter-weight warmer, apple hat; from rhubarb and apple to apple and quince, apple and raisin, blackberry and apple.

APPLE PIES

I prefer eating apples to cooking apples in an apple pie, and Cox's seem to have the best acid/sweet balance and texture for my palate. Worcester Pearmains, Reinettes and Ellison's Orange are delicious, too, when you can get them. The Americans favour Golden Delicious, but I happen not to agree. They are fine in tarts when you want something drier, but they don't have the strength of flavour and that's what you're looking for, particularly in a plain apple pie.

Apple Pie

SERVES 6
1.4kg/3lb apples
juice of a lemon
140g/5oz unrefined granulated
    sugar
½ tsp ground cinnamon

Pastry:
225g/8oz unsalted butter, cold
340g/12oz plain flour
1 dsrtsp unrefined caster
    sugar
1 tsp salt
an egg beaten with a little milk
    for glaze

First make the pastry. Cut the cold butter into small dice. Mix the flour, caster sugar and salt in a bowl and add the butter. Rub the butter in with your fingertips until the mixture has the texture of breadcrumbs, then add 3 tablespoons of ice-cold water and work quickly into a coherent dough. Divide the dough in half and wrap each flattened ball in clingfilm before putting it in the fridge for at least two hours, or overnight if it suits you.

Preheat the oven to 220°C/425°F/Gas 7. Peel, halve and core the apples, slice them thickly and put them in a bowl. Use your fingers to toss them in the lemon juice, all but a dessertspoon of the sugar and the cinnamon.

Roll out the first disc of pastry on a cold, floured surface to 30cm/12 inches in diameter, and drop it into your pie dish, allowing it to overlap the edge. Roll out the second disc, then pack the apples tightly into the pie, building them up into a dome shape in the middle of the dish. They will collapse in the cooking. Brush the edges of the pastry with cold water, then cover with the second sheet of pastry. Press down the edges and crimp them together. Cut a cross or slashes in the pie top to allow the steam to escape, brush the top with the beaten egg and milk glaze, and sprinkle over the rest of the sugar.

Bake for 25 minutes, then turn the heat down to 180°C/350°F/ Gas 4 and cook for a further 45 minutes. Cover the top with a sheet of greaseproof if the pastry is browning too quickly. What you want to make sure of is that the pastry underneath cooks through as well as the fruit. The pie is best eaten after it has been left to cool completely, so the fruit 'sets', which takes at least 3 hours. Then you may gently reheat the pie if you want to serve it hot. Serve with cream, clotted or Jersey; custard, homemade, naturally, or à la mode with a dollop of vanilla ice cream. There's nothing better.

You can either make dinky little individual puddings – I have small plastic lidded pudding basins for this and they are great for all things steamed – or you can make a seriously hat-sized hat. Here the cooking apple comes into its own. Go for the Bramley, and treat yourself to a pudding that is an unreconstructed rib-sticker, even without the mandatory clotted cream.

Apple Hat

SERVES 6
675g/1½lb Bramley or other
  cooking apples
40g/1½oz sultanas
75g/2½oz light muscovado
  sugar
3 cloves
½tsp ground cinnamon
½tsp ground dried ginger root
grated zest of an orange and
  the juice of half of it
55g/2oz butter, diced
1 tbsp clotted cream

Suet pastry:
225g/8oz self-raising flour
a pinch of salt
110g/4oz suet (shredded beef
  suet or the veggie kind)

Butter a 1-litre/2-pint pudding basin well. Sift the flour and salt into a large bowl, then stir in the suet and mix with enough cold water for the mixture to cohere into a light, soft dough. You don't want it damp and sticky, so 6–8 tablespoons of water should do it. Knead the dough lightly, then roll it out on a floured surface. Divide into two-thirds and one-third and line the pudding basin with the larger piece.

Peel, core and slice the apples and add them to the basin. Gently mix the sultanas, sugar and spices and add them, then the orange zest, juice and finely diced butter. Cover the top with the remaining circle of rolled-out suet, damping the edges and pressing them together well.

Cover with a piece of pleated greaseproof paper topped with a piece of pleated foil. Tie these on around the rim of the pudding basin, attaching a string handle with which you can remove the pudding basin from the pot. Place in a large pot with simmering water up to the middle of basin, cover and simmer for 2–2½ hours. Turn out on to a warm plate. If you feel like it, take out a piece of suet crust from the top of the hat and spoon in the clotted cream. Serve hot with more cream and muscovado sugar to sprinkle.

Apple and Raisin Pie

SERVES 8

20 Cox's apples or Reinettes

110g/4oz unrefined caster
  sugar

grated zest of half a lemon

110g/4oz unsalted butter

110g/4oz seedless organic
  raisins

demerara sugar

225g/8oz puff pastry
  (see p.141)

a beaten egg white

Peel, core and quarter the apples, slice them thinly and put them into a bowl. Sprinkle the apples with the caster sugar and lemon zest and mix them thoroughly with your hands. Melt the butter and add it to the apples, turning everything as you go. Finally add the raisins.

Preheat the oven to 230°C/450°F/Gas 8. Roll out the pastry thinly, cutting strips from it to put around the rim of the dish. Scrape the fruit and juices from the bowl into the pie dish, mounding them up towards the centre. Brush the pastry rim with the lightly beaten egg white. Lay the pastry sheet over the top and press it down. Use the tines of a fork to decorate the edge and cut loosely around the overhang. Slash a central hole in the top, brush the top with egg white and sprinkle over a little extra sugar. I think demerara works best with raisins.

Cook at the high temperature for 15 minutes, during which time the pastry will rise and turn golden brown. Lower the heat to 170°C/325°F/Gas 3 and continue to cook for another 15–20 minutes. Serve hot or warm with lashings of thin pouring cream.

There's rhubarb and ginger, rhubarb and orange – with or without honey – and the perhaps less well-known marriage of rhubarb and apple. I think this last partnership is every bit as successful, and the apple has the merit of somehow reducing and softening the acidity of the rhubarb in a really unexpected and delicious way. Allowing the fruits to begin to bleed into the dusky muscovado sugar before cooking is something you should try and leave time for. Take the time, too, to experiment, as I have, with a little church window lattice or the like, so your troughers can gaze upon what they are about to receive in all its day-glo pink prettiness. It does not, after all, demand a high degree of artistry to cut a few rough diamonds!

Rhubarb and Apple Pie

SERVES 6

1 bunch of rhubarb, washed and chopped into short lengths
4–6 eating apples depending on size, peeled, cored and sliced (Cox's are best)
140g/5oz or to taste muscovado sugar
shortcrust pastry made with 285g/10oz plain flour and 140g/5oz unsalted butter (see p.141)
beaten egg for glaze

In a large bowl, mix the rhubarb, apples and sugar together with your fingers. Leave for 20 minutes or so for the juices to begin to run.

Preheat the oven to 200°C/400°F/Gas 6. Pack the pie dish tightly with fruit, mounding it up in the centre in the usual way. Roll out the pastry. Cut off a strip and attach it to the rim of the dish, brushing the rim with water first. Brush the strip with water and cover the dish with the sheet of pastry. Drape it loosely rather than stretched taut, as there is always some shrinkage. If you feel like it, use a sharp knife point to cut out diamond shapes as in the photograph. Brush the pastry with beaten egg and place the pie in the oven for 20 minutes. Turn the heat down to 190°C/375°F/Gas 5 and continue to cook for another 20 minutes, when the pie should be golden and the fruit cooked through. Serve warm with cream or custard.

This is my take on the signature pie of the Little Pie Company of the Big Apple, the one that made them famous, the only recipe they will not give out and that doesn't grace the pages of their book. I had heard about them from a publisher I met in New York, but it wasn't until the lovely Rob said he knew where their headquarters were in the Meatpacking District, and why didn't we take a walk down there, that I discovered this fantastic enterprise. They make pies as good as the best homemade ones, with all the care, attention to detail and passion for good-quality ingredients that the best cooks share. They sent me away with their sour cream apple and walnut pie, and a peach pie. I then started agonizing about just how they made the apple one, which is the last word in scrumptiousness. Having eaten it warm for supper, Rob insisted that I try it cold for breakfast. My credulity stretched beyond all reason, my mistrust of American taste at an all-time high, I remained as passive as I could in the matter until it was spoon-fed me. Was it good? The best breakfast you could imagine. I went back for more. We finished it. Though the cynics among you would probably say its merits A.M. would have a lot to do with who was spoon feeding it to you. And now I could eat it at home if I dared, though I've no idea, despite three attempts to get close to the original, if the Little Pie Company would approve of my rendering.

Sour Cream Apple and Walnut Pie

Preheat the oven to 200°C/400°F/Gas 6. Grease a pie dish with butter, then line it with two-thirds of the rolled-out shortcrust pastry. Let the overhang hang loose for the moment.

Peel, core and thinly slice the apples. Toss them into a bowl with a small scattering of sugar and the soured cream, then mix with your hands until everything is well amalgamated. Pile this mixture into the pastry base, packing it tightly and mounding it up towards the centre.

For the topping, process the sugars, small bits of cold butter, syrup and flour together. Add the walnuts when you have stopped the processing and stir them in. Take lumps of the mixture on the palm of one hand and flatten them out with the other palm, so you have a flattened layer rather than a crumble top, and cover the surface of the apples bit by bit. Join the topping to the pastry edge before you cut off the pastry overhang.

SERVES 6–8

10 large eating apples, I prefer the tartness of Cox's to the Golden Delicious the Americans like

a little light brown muscovado sugar

142ml/5fl oz carton soured cream

Topping:

110g/4oz sugar, half light muscovado and half molasses

110g/4oz unsalted butter

a large tbsp golden syrup

55g/2oz flour

85g/3oz walnuts, bashed into small bits

shortcrust pastry made with 225g/8oz flour and 110g/4oz unsalted butter (see p.140)

Cook for 20 minutes before turning the temperature down to 180°C/350°F/Gas 4 and cooking for another 30–40 minutes. Check that the top layer is not darkening too much and if it is, cover with a layer of greaseproof or foil and continue cooking. The pie will smell ready when it is ready. I am of the firm belief that apple pie is best when left to cool for at least 3 hours after cooking, so if you want it warm or hot, work out your cooking times accordingly and reheat very gently. Warm and à la mode, with homemade vanilla ice cream, is the business, but even I would not suggest that for breakfast.

Quinces go beautifully with apple, adding another dimension to a pie, with their scented graininess and wonderful deep ruby colour. This is a perfect late autumn/early winter pudding. The quinces have to be grated, since even small chunks take aeons longer to cook than the apple.

Apple and Quince Pie

SERVES 6
560g/1¼lb Bramley or other
    cooking apples
1 large quince
unrefined granulated sugar
about 290ml/10fl oz water
a sheet of puff pastry (see
    p.141) or 225g/8oz short
    crust pastry (see p. 140)
sprinkling of demerara sugar

Preheat the oven to 200°C/400°F/Gas 6. Peel, core and slice the apples, then peel, core and grate the quince. Fill the pie dish with the fruit, sprinkling sugar over each layer, and mounding it up towards the centre of the dish. Pour the water into the dish to come half way up the fruit.

Roll out the pastry. Cut off a strip and attach it to the rim of the dish, brushing the rim with water first. Brush the strip with water and cover the dish with the sheet of pastry, cutting off all the overhanging bits. Crimp the edges, brush the top with water and strew over the demerara sugar. Bake for 20 minutes before turning the temperature down to 190°C/375°F/Gas 5 and cooking for a further 20 minutes. Eat warm or hot with lashings of cream.

I have adapted this from the Little Pie Company's book, *Pies and other Dessert Favorites*, published by HarperPerennial. Just make sure you use a good, strong Cheddar like Montgomery or Quicke's for this lovely sweet/savoury pie, an autumn dish which is baked on Thanksgiving Day in America.

Cheddar Crust Apple Pie

SERVES 6

7 large Granny Smith or Cox's
  apples
2 tbsp freshly squeezed lemon
  juice
85g/3oz unrefined sugar
110g/4oz flour
½ tsp ground cinnamon
a pinch of salt
55g/2oz unsalted butter,
  softened
beaten egg for glaze

Cheddar pastry:
225g/8oz flour
pinch of salt
110g/4oz unsalted butter
55g/2oz very cold lard
100g/3½oz strong mature
  Cheddar, coarsely grated

For the pastry, put the sieved flour and salt, chopped cold butter and lard in the food processor and blitz briefly before adding the cheese. With the machine running, add a tablespoon or two of water, just to the point at which the dough coheres. Wrap the ball of dough in clingfilm and refrigerate for a couple of hours before using.

Preheat the oven to 220°C/425°F/Gas 7. Peel, core and slice the apples thinly and toss them in a bowl with the lemon juice. Stir all but a dessertspoon of the sugar with the flour, cinnamon and salt, add to the apple slices and toss to coat.

Divide the dough into two pieces, one slightly larger than the other, and roll out the larger one. Line a greased shallow pie plate with the pastry, then pile in the apples, mounding them up towards the centre. Dot the filling with butter. Trim the bottom crust to give you a 0.5cm/¼in overhang. Roll out the second piece of dough and spread it over the top of the pie, allowing a 2cm/¾in overhang. Fold the top crust under the edge of the bottom crust and flute the edges, pressing them together with your fingers. Make slashes in the middle of the crust and bake in the oven for 20 minutes. Reduce the temperature to 190°C/375°F/Gas 5 and continue to bake until the pie is turning golden and the juices are bubbling.

Ten minutes before the end of the cooking time, brush the top with beaten egg and sprinkle over the remaining spoonful of sugar. This is what the Americans do. I think sprinkling over a handful of coarsely grated Cheddar is a much better idea. Let the pie cool on a wire rack before serving it warm or at room temperature.

First pick your blackberries. This is THE autumn pie, fruited with the very best of pie-fellows, the blackberry and the apple; a pie that evokes more memories than any other at this time of year. Think of winey-stained fingers and mouths; blackberries collapsing and bleeding their juices in your basket as you prick and sting and stretch and reach, the biggest, blackest, most glowing berries always just beyond your reach. Think of the childish joy in eating more off the tangles of thorny stems than ever get into the basket. Think of seeds stuck in teeth, berry turning apple deep purple, the heavenly smell as the hot juices run out from under the steaming crisp crust.

Quantities here are not a fixed thing. They're more to do with what you've picked, so go with what you've got and use the recipe below as a guideline.

Blackberry and Apple Pie

SERVES 6

14 sharp eating apples, peeled cored and sliced
450g/1lb blackberries, the red and the prickles discarded
110g/4oz, or to taste, light muscovado or unrefined granulated sugar
2 tsp cornflour
shortcrust pastry made with 225g/8oz flour and 110g/4oz unsalted butter (see p.140)
beaten egg for glaze

Preheat the oven to 200°C/400°F/Gas 6. Throw the apples and blackberries into a huge bowl, scatter over the sugar and sifted cornflour, then turn the fruit gently with your fingers. Leave to stand for 20–30 minutes, then hurl everything into the pie dish.

Roll out the pastry and cut off a strip. Wet the rim of the dish with water, then stick on the strip of pastry. Wet the pastry strip and cover with the sheet of pastry, crimping the edges together with the tines of a fork. Decorate with a few pastry blackberries and the odd apple if you feel inspired. Brush with beaten egg, cut a central hole for the steam to escape from and cook for 20 minutes. Turn the heat down to 190°C/375°F/Gas 5 and cook for a further 20 minutes until the top is burnished. Serve hot or warm with lashings of cream or custard. Great cold too, with rivulets of purple juice staining the cream.

There are black bottoms and Mississippi muds, key limes and Kentucky sweet potato, sour-cream apple-and-walnut and the plain perfection of peach, pecan, cherry, blueberry, pumpkin or old-fashioned apple. 'As American as apple pie' goes the well-worn saying, but the American tradition of sweet pies is unarguably all their own, and even if we lose a little sweetness along the way and pass on the airy clouds of sugared chantilly cream, we all know and love a classic American pie. Here are some of my absolute favourites, not by any means the whole repertoire, but the Fourth of July and Thanksgiving specials; the event pies and the non-event, everyday, down-home comforters; the plain-and-simple and the dazzling; a little chapter and verse from across the pond.

AMERICAN PIES

Just the name, peach pie, is so emotive with its alliterative, run-off-the-tongue sort of sound, conjuring up perfect summers, clear blue skies, scented, sticky ripeness, the glut of the season, the fullness of flavour of what is the ultimate in sensual fruits. I prefer mine white to gaudy orange, they are the more delicate and better flavoured of the two peaches — assuming the pedigree of the variety and its ripeness, of course. Never be lured into buying underripe. They NEVER ripen off the branch, but just turn to cotton wool; and underripe peaches, no matter what you think, never soften in the cooking either. They remain hard, acidic and thoroughly unpleasant.

You can go one of two ways here. Either make a double crust pie with a bottom crust and a lattice top, or stick to just a shortcrust top. So either go 340g/12oz flour to 170g/6oz butter for a double crust, or use slightly over half these measurements to be on the generous side for a single crust.

Peach Pie

SERVES 6–8
8 large ripe peaches
juice of a lemon
4 tbsp sugar
1–1½ tbsp cornflour
½ tsp ground cinnamon
a little extra sugar, demerara
    or granulated
shortcrust pastry (see above
    and p.140)
beaten egg for glaze

Submerge the peaches, one at a time, in scalding water for 30 seconds to a minute. Pierce with a knife point, peel off the skin and then halve and stone the peaches. Cut each half into four slices. Put the slices into a large bowl and squeeze lemon juice over them to prevent discoloration. Mix together the sugar, sifted cornflour and cinnamon and combine with the peaches. Let them stand for 15 minutes or so.

Preheat the oven to 220°C/425°F/Gas 7. Line the greased pie dish with shortcrust pastry if you are going down that route, then throw in the peach mixture. Roll out the rest of the pastry into a circle and cut out lattice strips. Brush them with beaten egg and strew them with a little sugar. Place the strips on top of the pie, pressing them into the bottom crust edges, and bake for 20 minutes. Reduce the heat to 180°C/350°F/Gas 4 and continue to bake for 40 minutes or until the pastry is browned and the juices breaking through and bubbling. Let the pie cool completely on a wire rack.

Serve at room temperature with homemade vanilla ice cream — even better if you've stirred some pralinéed almonds into the ice cream; they are a perfect foil for the peaches.

With its gloopy, butterscotch middle, soft nuttiness and crisp pastry, this is the perfect pie for a good Sunday lunch or a special occasion. You can gild the lily and add a cloudy oval of marshmallowy meringue to each portion, or you can leave well alone, save for the cold stream of pouring cream that matches ivory with fudgy, caramel brown.

Pecan Pie

SERVES 6–8

200g/7oz dark muscovado sugar
85g/3oz unsalted butter
240ml/8fl oz single cream
2 heaped tbsp cornflour
1 tsp pure vanilla extract
2 egg yolks
110g/4oz pecan nuts
shortcrust pastry made with 110g/4oz flour and 55g/2oz unsalted butter (see p.140)

Meringue top (optional):
3 egg whites
55g/2oz unrefined caster sugar

Preheat the oven to 200°C/400°F/Gas 6. Line a greased 23cm/9in tart tin with the rolled-out pastry, then bake blind for 20 minutes (see p.140). Turn the oven down to 180°C/350°F/Gas 4. Remove the greaseproof paper and beans and return the pastry to the oven for a further 5 minutes.

Pour the sugar, butter and cream into the top of a double boiler, sift over the cornflour and whisk over a gentle heat until the mixture thickens and is wondrously free of lumps. Off the heat, add the vanilla extract and whisk in the egg yolks, one at a time. Then stir in the pecan nuts and scrape the mixture into the pastry shell.

If you're adding meringue, whisk the egg whites until stiff, add a third of the sugar and whisk again. Fold in the next third of sugar, pile the meringue on to the pecan filling and sprinkle over the remaining sugar. Bake at 180°C/350°F/Gas 4 for 20 minutes or until the meringue has bronzed and crisped to a crackling top. Remove from the oven and leave for a few minutes before serving.

I first wrote about this irresistible pudding in *The Art of the Tart*, having come across it browsing in Nach Waxman's wonderful cookbook shop, Kitchen Arts and Letters in New York. The pie has its roots in the Deep South and the legendary James Beard believed the first recipes date from around the turn of the 20th century. It is rich. Oh, yes. Its chocolate crumb crust is covered by a layer of darkly delicious chocolate pastry cream, signifying the black, swampy lowlands along the Mississippi River. A froth of rum-flavoured chiffon tops it like a light, low-lying cloud.

Black Bottom Cream Pie

SERVES 6–8

Chocolate crumb crust:
110g/4oz plain flour
3 tsp Green and Black's organic cocoa powder
1 heaped dsrtsp unrefined icing sugar
55g/2oz unsalted cold butter cut into small pieces
1 egg yolk
1 egg white

Chocolate pastry cream:
4 egg yolks
4 tbsp unrefined sugar
4 tsp cornflour
500ml/18fl oz milk, scalded
1 tbsp dark rum
1 vanilla pod, split
55g/2oz best bitter chocolate, broken into small pieces

Meringue chiffon topping:
1½ tsp gelatine
100ml/3½ fl oz double cream, whipped
2 tbsp dark rum
1 tsp vanilla extract
3 egg whites
6 tbsp unrefined icing sugar
½ tsp cream of tartar

First make the crust. Sift the flour, cocoa and sugar into the bowl of a food processor, add the butter and whizz briefly. Add the egg yolk and a tablespoon or two of ice-cold water, then process again until the point at which the pastry coheres. Wrap in clingfilm and refrigerate for at least an hour. Preheat the oven to 200°C/400°F/Gas 6. Roll out the pastry on some flour sifted with a little extra cocoa powder and line the greased tart tin. Bake the crust blind for 20 minutes (see p.140). Remove the beans, prick the base with a fork and brush with egg white. Return to the oven for 5 minutes.

For the chocolate pastry cream, whisk the egg yolks and sugar together thoroughly, then sift in the cornflour and blend until smooth. Whisk in the hot milk, return the mixture to the pan and stir it over a gentle heat until thickened. Add the rum, the scraped-out seeds of the vanilla pod and the broken chocolate, then stir until melted and smooth. Scrape the chocolate cream into the cooled pastry case.

For the topping, dissolve the gelatine in 2 tablespoons of water. Add it to 1cm/½ in of simmering water in a small saucepan and dissolve fully over a gentle heat for 3–5 minutes. Stir this into the whipped, but not stiff, cream and blend together. Add the rum and vanilla extract, then cool over ice or briefly in the deep freeze until the mixture has thickened but is not freezing. Whisk the egg whites until stiff, add one-third of the sugar and whisk again. Add another third of the sugar and the cream of tartar and whisk until glossy. Fold the remaining sugar in gently with a metal spoon, then fold the meringue into the gelatine mixture and dollop it on to the tart. Refrigerate for at least a couple of hours. You can decorate with grated chocolate or a sparing sifting of cocoa powder if you feel like it.

Morello cherries are the ultimate, but sourcing them is as difficult as panning for gold these days. Just find the best cherries you can, and a good catapult of a stoner to pit them with, a messily satisfying and repetitive job. The crunch of a demerara sugar top and a solid scoop of clotted cream make this pie for me. The cornflour is needed to thicken the weeping cherry juices and stop them from flooding the crust.

Sugar-Topped Cherry Pie

SERVES 6

750g/1lb 10oz cherries,
    pre-stoned weight
1–2 tbsp Kirsch
2 dsrtsp cornflour
110g/4oz unrefined sugar
1 tbsp demerara sugar
shortcrust pastry made with
    285g/10oz flour and 140g/5oz
    unsalted butter (see p.140)
beaten egg for glaze

Stone the cherries, then macerate them in a large bowl with the Kirsch and sugar for an hour or so. Pour off the juice that has collected into a smaller bowl and stir in the sifted cornflour to thicken it. Return the thickened juice to the cherries.

Preheat the oven to 200°C/400°F/Gas 6. Divide the pastry into roughly two-thirds and one-third. Roll out the larger piece for the base of the pie and drop it into a greased pie dish. Pour in the cherry mixture. Roll out the second piece of pastry and place it over the cherries, crimping the edges together well with the tines of a fork. Brush the top with beaten egg, then throw on the demerara. Make a couple of slashes in the crust for the steam to escape through and bake the pie for about 40 minutes, or until the top has browned. Serve warm or at room temperature with clotted cream, or à la mode with homemade vanilla ice cream.

Spicy, nutty, fruity, this is a delight of a pie. If you omit the nuts and spices it becomes Kentucky Pie.

Jefferson Davis Pie

SERVES 6–8

110g/4oz unsalted butter
225g/8oz light brown
  muscovado sugar
4 egg yolks
2 tbsp flour
1 tsp ground cinnamon
½ tsp allspice
1 tsp grated nutmeg
240ml/8fl oz double cream
85g/3oz dates, chopped
85g/3oz raisins
85g/3oz pecan nuts, chopped
shortcrust pastry made with
  110g/4oz flour and 55g/2oz
  unsalted butter (see p.140)

Roll out the pastry and line a 23cm/9in tart tin. Preheat the oven to 200°C/400°F/Gas 6 and bake the pastry case blind for 20 minutes (see p.140). Remove the beans and greaseproof and return the pastry to the oven for 5 minutes until pale gold in colour.

Turn the oven down to 170°C/325°F/Gas 3. Cream the butter and sugar together in a large bowl, then beat in the egg yolks one at a time. Mix together the flour, cinnamon, allspice and nutmeg and add them to the bowl, then stir in the cream, dates, raisins and pecan nuts. Scrape the filling into the cooked pie shell and bake for about 30 minutes until set.

You can eat this pie warm, as is, or cover with meringue made with 3 egg whites and 85g/3oz unrefined caster sugar in the usual way. Bake the pie for a further 15–20 minutes until the meringue is crisp and golden.

This unusual and delicious recipe is adapted from a traditional favourite of the Shakers, a religious group from Ohio. It has a light and luscious lemony flavour and all the texture of the lemons with none of the bitterness of the pith.

Shaker or Ohio Lemon Pie

SERVES 4–6
zest of 2 lemons
4 lemons, skin and white pith
   and pips removed and the
   flesh very thinly sliced
55g/2oz plain flour sifted
340–400g/12–13oz unrefined
   caster sugar
4 eggs
40g/1½oz unsalted butter,
   melted
2 tbsp double cream

Pastry:
340g/12oz flour
2 tbsp icing sugar
170g/6oz unsalted butter
1 egg yolk
beaten egg for glaze

Make the pastry by whizzing the sifted flour and icing sugar together in a food processor, then adding the cold butter in tiny dice. When the mixture resembles fine crumbs, add the egg yolk and two tablespoons of very cold water and process into a smooth ball. Wrap and refrigerate for 30 minutes to an hour.

Preheat the oven to 200°C/400°F/Gas 6. Place the lemon zest, lemon slices, flour, sugar, eggs, butter and cream in a bowl and stir to combine.

Divide the pastry into roughly two-thirds and one-third. Roll out the larger piece and line a greased pie dish. Stir the filling and pour it into the dish. Brush the rim of the pastry with water, roll out the second piece of pastry and place it over the base. Crimp the edges together and trim off the excess. Cut steam holes in the crust, brush the top with beaten egg and bake for 20 minutes. Turn the oven down to 180°C/350°F/Gas 4 and continue to bake the pie for another 30 minutes. Leave on a rack to cool, then serve with pouring cream.

This is my rendering of the American classic. It is difficult to find key lime juice, which is bottled in Key West in Florida and has a slightly fizzy, sherberty quality, but good organic limes make a great pie. I normally avoid any contact with condensed milk, but this pie needs it!

Key Lime Pie

SERVES 6–8
4 egg yolks
1 x 400g/13oz can sweetened
    condensed milk
1 tsp finely grated lime zest
150ml/5fl oz freshly squeezed
    lime juice
240ml/8fl oz double cream
1 tbsp unrefined caster sugar
fully baked shortcust pie shell
    in 23cm/9in tin (see p.140)

Preheat the oven to 180°C/350°F/Gas 4. Whisk together the egg yolks, condensed milk and half the lime zest, then slowly stir in the lime juice. Pour the mixture into the pastry shell and bake it for 20 minutes. Let the pie cool on a wire rack before refrigerating it for about 2 hours or until chilled.

Decorate the top with pinches of lime zest. If you want to go very rich, whip the double cream, fold in the sugar and the rest of the lime zest, then dollop it on top of the pie.

Nick and I met when he was my son's tutor at Eton. He's a cook of the keenest and most wanting-to-learn variety, with a huge collection of cookery books and wacky kitchen gadgets. He and his wife Sal have shared many a dinner with us in Somerset and Ireland, everything from langoustines straight out of Killary Bay to the New Year's goose. Here's Nick's condensed milk-free version of Key Lime Pie.

Nick Welsh's Key Lime Pie

SERVES 8
170g/6oz digestive biscuits,
    crushed to crumbs
85g/3oz butter, melted
55g/2oz sugar
4 whole eggs and 2 yolks
170g/6oz sugar
juice of 4 limes
grated zest of 2 limes
225g/8oz butter, diced
290ml/10fl oz whipping cream
1 tbsp clear honey

To make the base, mix together the biscuit crumbs, melted butter and 55g/2oz sugar. Using the back of a wooden spoon, press the mixture into the base of a 18cm/7in pie tin with a removable base.

Whisk together the whole eggs and yolks, sugar, lime juice and zest. Cook the mixture in a double boiler, the saucepan not resting in the water beneath and the water simmering gently, not boiling, until it thickens, stirring all the while. Off the heat whisk in the butter. Pour the filling into the crust and chill to set. Whip the cream until floppily stiff, add the honey and serve.

I remember the first blueberry doughnut I ever ate, warm from a Long Island diner, with my cousin David. He had, as usual, bought double the quantity any sane mortals could ever eat. And we scoffed the lot. I have tried and failed to replicate the experience ever since, the blueberryishness of the blueberries, the way they were suspended in a purple, fruity gloop which had none of the characteristics of a factory production line, any more than did the crisp fried doughnut with its damply gritty sugar coat. I don't even really like doughnuts as a rule, but blueberries are another matter and although there is a wonderful grower in Dorset, I think of blueberries and blueberry pie as essentially American.

Blueberry Pie

SERVES 6

675g/1½lb blueberries
85g/3oz sugar, or to taste
2 tbsp cornflour
½ tsp ground cinnamon
juice of half a lemon
30g/1oz unsalted butter, softened
demerara sugar to sprinkle
shortcrust pastry made with 285g/10oz flour and 140g/5oz unsalted butter (see p.140)
beaten egg for glaze

Tip the berries into a large bowl. Mix together the sugar, sifted cornflour and cinnamon and scatter them over the blueberries. Squeeze over the lemon juice and toss together. Leave the mixture to stand for at least 15 minutes so that all the flavours can develop.

Preheat the oven to 220°C/425°F/Gas 7. Divide the pastry into roughly two-thirds and one-third. Roll out the larger piece and line the bottom of a greased pie dish, then spoon in the blueberry mixture, mounding it up towards the middle. Dot with butter.

Top with the second piece of pastry and press both edges together. Cut any shapes you feel like into the top crust – it is rather quaint and pretty to be able to look down through the cut shapes into the fruity murk below.

Brush the pastry with beaten egg and bake for 15 minutes. Turn the oven temperature down to 190°C/375°F/Gas 5 and continue to bake for another 35 minutes. Ten minutes before the end of cooking time, brush the top with a little more beaten egg and strew with demerara. Let the pie cool completely before serving with cream.

If you can imagine a darkly cracked crust, intersected by parched fissures like mud baked in an equatorial sun, a scorched earth of a dish, then you would recognize the look of a Mississippi Mud Pie, with its surprisingly fondant-like centre underneath.

Mississippi Mud Pie

SERVES 6–8

225g/8oz unsalted butter
110g/4oz dark chocolate,
    minimum 70% cocoa solids
3 large eggs
1 tbsp espresso coffee
    granules dissolved in
    2 tbsp soured cream
170g/6oz granulated sugar
3 tbsp golden syrup
1 tsp pure vanilla extract
shortcrust pastry made with
    170g/6oz flour and 85g/3oz
    unsalted butter (see p.140)

Preheat the oven to 180°C/350°F/Gas 4. Line a 25cm/10in greased pie dish with the pastry and put it in the fridge. Melt the butter and chocolate in the top of a double boiler over gently simmering water. The base of the pan must not touch the water. Remove from the heat and continue to stir it as it begins to cool. In a KitchenAid or with a whisk, beat together the dissolved coffee granules, sugar, syrup and vanilla extract, then stir in the slightly cooled chocolate mixture. Pour into the pastry shell.

Bake in the oven for about 35 minutes, or until the filling puffs up and forms a crisp, cracked crust and the pastry is golden and cooked through. Cool on a wire rack, during which time the filling will deflate somewhat, but the inside will cool to a squidgy, creamy fudginess. Serve at room temperature slathered with whipped cream that you have beaten to a soft stiffness and added to an equal amount of strained yoghurt – turn a pot of yoghurt into a sieve lined with a J-cloth and set over a jug, then leave in the fridge overnight so that in the morning it is thick and drained of its liquid. Or just go for some really fine crème fraîche.

I found the recipe for Kentucky Sweet Potato Pie in the Little Pie Company's book that I mentioned in the apple chapter. On Thanksgiving last year I made it with a luminous, day-glo-orange red onion squash and it was utterly delicious – sweet and spicy without being cloying or just plain odd. Experiment with any squash you can find, as well as with sweet potatoes or the classic Thanksgiving and Halloween pumpkin. Just go easy on the sugar as the vegetables are so naturally sweet. I cut the LPC's sugar by half and it was perfect. I roasted the pumpkin in the oven in melon-sized wedges until soft when pierced with a skewer point – about 30 minutes.

Kentucky Sweet Potato or Pumpkin Pie

SERVES 6–8

about 675g/1½lb sweet potato, pumpkin or squash
240ml/8fl oz single cream
55g/2oz unsalted butter, softened
55g/2oz light muscovado sugar
2 large eggs
½ tsp ground cinnamon
½ tsp ground mace
½ tsp ground cloves
½ tsp ground ginger
1 tsp pure vanilla extract
½ tsp sea salt
shortcrust pastry made with 110g/4oz flour and 55g/2oz unsalted butter (see p.140)

Cut the pumpkin or sweet potato into full-length, melon-like wedges and remove the seeds if using pumpkin. Roast the slices on a baking tray in a hot oven for about 30 minutes.

Preheat the oven to 180°C/350°F/Gas 4. Stir the cream into the mashed pumpkin or sweet potato in a large bowl. In another bowl, or in a KitchenAid, cream together the butter and sugar until light and fluffy, then add the eggs, one at a time, beating them in as you go. Stir this mixture into the sweet potatoes and cream, then stir in the spices, vanilla extract and salt.

Line a 23cm/9in tart tin with pastry, then pour in the filling, spreading it into an even layer with a rubber spatula. Bake the pie for about an hour or until lightly browned and slightly puffed up. Let it cool on a rack before serving warm or at room temperature.

'Can she bake a cherry pie, Billy boy, Billy boy?'
This song wafts into my head whenever I think of
summer berry pies, sweet fruit pies, sharp, tangy
lemon or lime pies, airy chiffony clouds of meringue
pies. Who, after all, would have married a girl who
couldn't bake a pie before the food giants took baking
out of the home kitchen and into the realms of the
ready made, the world of gloopy, day-glo pie fillings
and sheets of grey, play-dough pastry?

Prinking and crimping, rolling and baking, cutting
and shaping, brushing and pasting – arcane repetitive
rituals they may be, but get back to them. They could,
after all, surprise you and give you as much pleasure
as they do your children or your grandchildren.
I always make a little extra pastry for precisely that
reason, so that my children can invent their own
miniature pies and rescue them, bronzed and
bubbling, from the heat of the oven, learning that
pastry is not the enemy and that pies are the ultimate
dish – comforting, good-natured, brim full of buried
treasure, the makers of memories.

SWEET PIES

Of all the summer pies, scented and sweet, tart and creamy, this is the dreamiest, and the intensity of both colour and flavour is matchless. I apply the same principles to this invincible marriage of berries as I do to summer puddings or sorbets, which is one-third redcurrants to two-thirds raspberries. The secret of the vibrant crimson juice, which hovers between thickness and thinness, is to strew the raspberries with sugar and let them begin to bleed while raw. That way you can mix the sugary juice with a little cornflour and redistribute it over the red orbs and berries before you cover them with pastry.

Raspberry and Redcurrant Pie

SERVES 6

450g/1lb raspberries

140g/5oz redcurrants stripped
    from their stems

110g/4oz or to taste unrefined
    granulated sugar

1 tbsp cornflour

demerara sugar

shortcrust pastry made with
    340g/12oz flour and 170g/6oz
    unsalted butter (see p.140)

beaten egg for glaze

Throw the fruit into a bowl, then scatter over most of the unrefined sugar and gently turn the berries so that the sugar can permeate more easily. Leave the fruit like this for as long as it takes to create a little puddle of liquor, about 20 minutes. Pour the liquid over a tablespoon of cornflour in a bowl and stir until the cornflour has dissolved and is smooth rather than lumpy.

Preheat the oven to 200°C/400°F/Gas 6. Line a pie dish with half the pastry, then scatter a little more sugar over the base before piling in the fruit. Roll out the second piece of pastry, pour the cornflour juice on to the fruit and put on the pastry topcoat. Seal the edges together with the tines of a fork and cut a cross in the centre for the steam to escape through. Brush with beaten egg.

Put the pie in the oven for 20 minutes, then remove, scatter over a handful of demerara sugar and return to the oven for 35–40 minutes at 180°C/350°F/Gas 4. Let the pie rest for 10 minutes before you cut into it. Serve with Jersey cream.

This is a classic, American-style fruit pie with a free-form rough crust that you wrap unsymmetrically and messily around a pile of sugared fruit. It involves no crimping, primping and decorating. It simply and unshowily displays the talents of the ingredients, fruit and pastry, and brings them together, making a virtue of inelegance. You may use any fruit or combination of fruit you choose, though I think plums, damsons and greengages are pretty damn fine.

Bottom-Crust Fruit Pie

SERVES 6

750g/1lb 10oz fruit, plums,
    damsons, greengages,
    gooseberries, blackberry
    or apple
75–85g/2½–3oz sugar
    depending on the sweetness
    of the fruit
egg white to glaze and a little
    extra sugar
shortcrust pastry made with
    225g/8oz flour and 110g/4oz
    unsalted butter, or, better
    still, half butter, half lard
    (see p.140)

Cut plums or greengages in half and remove the stones. Damsons you have to leave unstoned; gooseberries should be topped and tailed; apples peeled, quartered, cored and cut into chunks.

Preheat the oven to 200°C/400°F/Gas 6. Roll the pastry out into a large circle, about 30cm/12in in diameter, and flip it from the rolling pin into a greased baking tin. Hurl the fruit into the middle of it in a reckless pile and sprinkle over the sugar. Fold over the edges of the pastry as far as they will go without stretching them, fatal to pastry which is shrinking by nature. The edges should very definitely not meet in the middle. Brush the pastry with egg white and scatter over a little more sugar, demerara if you prefer.

Bake for 20 minutes, then turn the oven temperature down to 180°C/350°F/Gas 4 and bake for a further 25–30 minutes until bubbling with juices and golden brown.

The English have treacle tart, the Americans pecan pie. This walnut pie follows both traditions – it is tooth-achingly, brain-searingly sweet, but the nuts manage to cut the sugar far more convincingly than the breadcrumbs we use in our sweetest of sweets. You can always grate in a little eating apple if you feel like a second cut of sharpness.

Walnut Pie

SERVES 6–8

110g/4oz light muscovado sugar

110g/4oz unsalted butter

3 eggs

4 heaped tbsp golden syrup

2 heaped tbsp black treacle

the zest and juice of 1 organic lemon

225g/8oz walnuts, cut into small nubbly chunks

shortcrust pastry made with 110g/4oz flour and 55g/2oz unsalted butter (see p.140)

Preheat the oven to 200°C/400°F/Gas 6. Line a 23cm/9in tart tin with shortcrust and bake the pastry blind in the usual way (see p.140). Turn the oven temperature down to 180°C/350°F/Gas 4.

Cream together the sugar and butter until light and fluffy, then beat in the eggs one at a time. Warm the syrup and treacle until they're just runny and stir them into the butter and sugar with the zest, juice and nuts.

Scrape the mixture into the pastry case and bake for about 45 minutes until dark brown and puffed up. Eat warm or cold with lashings of pouring cream.

Plum and Walnut Pie

SERVES 6

675g/1½lb plums, halved, stoned and chopped

110g/4oz light muscovado sugar

110g/4oz chopped walnuts

1–2 tsp ground cinnamon

grated zest of 1 organic lemon and 1 organic orange

55g/2oz butter, melted

shortcrust pastry made with 340g/12oz flour and 170g/6oz unsalted butter (see p.140)

beaten egg or egg white to glaze and a little extra sugar

Plums and walnuts work beautifully together, with a little cinnamon and butter to distract from the sharpness of the fruit.

Preheat the oven to 190°C/375°F/Gas 5. Divide the pastry into roughly two-thirds and one-third, roll out the larger piece and line a 23cm/9in pie dish. Mix the plums with the sugar, walnuts, cinnamon and grated zests and scrape them into the pastry case. Pour over the melted butter.

Roll out the other piece of pastry and cover the fruit, crimping the pastry edges together. Cut a central hole for the steam to escape through. Brush the top with beaten egg or egg white and sprinkle over a little extra sugar. Bake for about an hour and serve warm with cream or homemade vanilla custard.

A lovely fudgy, creamy pie, with a scrumptious combination of banana and walnut that isn't half bad in a white, heavily buttered sarnie either! This pie is a serious crowd pleaser in the minors department, as is the Canadian Pie below.

Banana and Walnut Pie

SERVES 6
225g/8oz best fresh cream
  cheese or mascarpone
75g/2½oz light muscovado
  sugar
1 egg, beaten
3 or 4 bananas
75g/2½oz chopped walnuts
zest of a lemon and a
  teaspoon or two of juice
a little milk
unrefined caster sugar
225g/8oz puff pastry
  (see p.141)

Preheat the oven to 210°C/425°F/Gas 7. Line a 23cm/9in greased tart case with a little over half the pastry and prick it all over with a fork. Put the cream cheese and sugar into a large bowl and cream them together, then amalgamate with the beaten egg. Slice the bananas and add them with the walnuts, zest and juice, stirring them all in together.

Spoon the mixture into the tart case and smooth the top with a palette knife. Cover with the top circle of pastry and crimp the edges together with the tines of a fork. Brush the top with a little milk, sprinkle over a bit of caster sugar and bake for 25–35 minutes until puffed up and golden. Serve hot or cold with pouring cream.

Canadian Pie

SERVES 6
4 heaped tbsp maple syrup
1½ tbsp runny honey
30g/1oz unsalted butter
1 egg, beaten
2–3 tbsp double cream
140g/5oz currants
30g/1oz ground almonds
¼–½tsp mixed spice
¼ tsp grated nutmeg
grated zest of a lemon
3 tsp lemon juice
shortcrust pastry made with
  110g/4oz flour and 55g/2oz
  unsalted butter (see p.140)

Meringue:
3 egg whites
55g/2oz caster sugar

Preheat the oven to 190°C/375°F/Gas 5. Roll out the pastry and line a 23cm/9in tart tin. Bake the pastry blind for 15 minutes (see p.140). Remove the beans, prick the base with a fork and brush with beaten egg. Return to the oven for 5 minutes.

Heat the maple syrup, honey and butter in a pan until liquid. Remove from the heat and stir in the beaten egg and cream. Mix all the other filling ingredients together in a bowl, pour in the golden syrup mixture and stir well. Pour into the pastry case.

For the meringue, whisk 3 egg whites until stiff, add one-third of the caster sugar and whisk again. Add another third of the sugar and fold it in gently with a metal spoon. Spread the meringue over the filling and sprinkle with the remaining sugar. Put into the oven for 20 minutes or until beautifully browned and crunchy on top.

Summer berries make the most magical pies and gooseberries are one of the best, either sweet scented with a little muscaty elderflower or drenched in demerara sugar. For some reason, the gooseberry, like rhubarb, is brought to life with a good puddle of homemade custard; perhaps it is the soothing nature of this British emollient that does it, dampening the acidic bite, the fruit's sharp-edged weapon, and acting as a perfect foil. And the combination works just as well with a gooseberry fool, which I feel should always be custard rather than cream based, with hidden jewels of gooseberries which you splurt into the custard with the tines of a fork.

Gooseberry Pie

SERVES 6

675g/1½lb gooseberries, topped and tailed

110g/4oz or to taste demerara sugar, the berries can be very sharp at the beginning of the season

2 dsrtsp cornflour

2 tbsp Rock's elderflower cordial, or your own homemade (optional)

30g/1oz unsalted butter

shortcrust pastry made with 225g/8oz flour and 110g/4oz unsalted butter (see p.140)

beaten egg for glaze

Put the gooseberries in a large bowl and throw over nearly all of the demerara sugar. Sift over the cornflour and add the elderflower if you are using it. Leave to macerate for at least 15 minutes, then pour the contents into the bottom of your pie dish. Dot with butter.

Preheat the oven to 200°C/400°F/Gas 6. Brush the rim of the pie dish with water and stick a strip of pastry around it. Brush the strip with more water and stick the pastry top to it, crimping the edges together and decorating if you feel like it. If you want to cut a shape out of the top of the pastry, do it before you lower it on to the pie dish. Brush the top with beaten egg and sprinkle the rest of the demerara over the exposed fruit.

Cook for 15 minutes, then turn the heat down to 180°C/350°F/Gas 5 and continue to cook for 30 minutes, until the fruit is cooked through and bubbling and the sugar has turned a dark treacly brown. Serve hot or warm with homemade custard or cream if you prefer.

I guess this is a pie originally inspired by the classic lemon meringue. It's no less good for being an obvious idea – sharp fruit offset by sweet meringue, the same principle as the custard with the plain gooseberry pie on page 124. The meringue used here is unusual in that there is an egg yolk folded into the white, but the dry, crunchy texture works beautifully with the sharp, seedy-textured fruit.

Gooseberry Meringue Pie or Rhubarb Meringue Pie

SERVES 6

450g/1lb gooseberries, topped and tailed, or the same of rhubarb cut into short lengths
55g/2oz butter
2 tbsp demerara sugar
3 large egg whites
1 egg yolk
1 tbsp flour
85g/3oz unrefined sugar
shortcrust pastry made with 110g/4oz flour and 55g/2oz unsalted butter (see p.140)

Bake the pastry blind in a 23cm/9in tart tin (see p.140). Melt the butter in a large, heavy-bottomed frying pan, then add the demerara sugar. When it has turned to liquid caramel, throw in the fruit in a single layer. Cover and cook briefly, until the skin changes colour if you are using gooseberries, then remove the pan from the heat. Cool the fruit mixture and check the sugar levels for taste before putting it into the pastry case.

Preheat the oven to 140°C/275°F/Gas 1. Whisk the egg whites stiffly, then fold in the yolk, followed by the flour and sugar sifted together. Cover the whole of the top of the pie with meringue, then bake in the oven for 40 minutes, until the top is cooked and golden. Serve hot, warm or cold with pouring cream.

Suet crust is the easiest of pastries to make and in the case of this pudding it should be rolled out good and thin and steamed to a crisp crust. When you break through it, out bursts a dam of thick buttery juices with a flood of yellow-green berries. All you need then is a golden tide of hot vanilla-tinged, homemade custard. A trencherman's pudding.

Steamed Gooseberry Pudding

SERVES 6
450g/1lb gooseberries, topped
  and tailed
110g/4oz demerara sugar
55g/2oz unsalted butter

Suet crust:
225g/8oz self-raising flour
110g/4oz suet, beef or
  vegetarian, chopped fine
½ tsp sea salt

To make the crust, sift the self-raising flour into a large bowl, add the suet and salt, and mix together thoroughly. Stir in about 8 tablespoons of ice-cold water to make a soft but not sticky dough. Add a little more flour if the dough sticks to your fingers. Shape it into a ball, then roll it out on a floured surface to the size of a large plate. Cut a quarter out of it to keep for the lid. Butter the pudding basin, then drop in the large piece of dough so that it comes just over the rim.

Mix the gooseberries with the sugar and butter, then pour them into the crust. Roll out the remaining dough into a circle for the lid and place it about 2.5cm/1in below the rim of the bowl to allow for the pudding to rise. Moisten the edges of the of the bottom crust first so it will adhere to the lid.

Make a cover for the pudding with a layer of greaseproof and a layer of foil with a single pleat in the middle of each. Tie string around the base of the rim of the basin and fashion a simple handle over the top. Put the pudding in a large, heavy, lidded pan, with boiling water up to its middle, and steam gently for a couple of hours. Check every so often and top up the water if you need to. An extra half an hour won't cause any grief.

There would be no point in giving you a recipe for mince pies if you're going to buy jars of mincemeat and merely spoon it into your pastry. By way of encouragement – other than that the taste is infinitely superior – let me tell you it takes longer to assemble the ingredients than it does to weigh, stir and bottle, so get to it, no excuses, or get a child numerate enough to weigh things to do it for you. If you tire of the traditional versions, make mincemeat bateaux or a huge tart which you can lattice or cover completely.

Mince Pies

MAKES TWO LARGE
JARS OF MINCEMEAT
about 340g/12oz each of
    organic sultanas, raisins
    and currants
170g/6oz blanched almonds,
    finely chopped
3 Cox's apples cut into dolls'
    size dice
400g/13oz dark muscovado
    sugar
200g/7oz organic mixed peel,
    finely chopped
grated zest and juice of
    1½ organic lemons and the
    zest of 1 organic orange
1 tsp nutmeg, grated
¼ tsp each ground cloves and
    cinnamon
⅛ tsp ground mace and dried
    root ginger
170g/6oz beef or vegetarian
    suet
4 tbsp dark rum
120ml/4fl oz Somerset Cider
    Brandy or Calvados

Pastry:
shortcrust pastry made with
    450g/1lb flour and 225g/8oz
    unsalted butter (see p.140)
beaten egg for glaze

To make the mincemeat, mix all the ingredients together in a colossal bowl. Decant into sterilized jars, cover and keep. Turn the jars upside down every so often so that the alcohol permeates every ingredient as much as possible. I am eating last year's mincemeat this year and it hasn't suffered in the least.

To make mince pies, fill the little patty tins with pastry and spoon in mincemeat generously. Brush the pastry rims with water and stick the pastry hats on, pressing down firmly all the way round the edge. Brush with beaten egg, prick a cross for the steam to escape through and cook in a hot oven, 200°C/400°F/Gas 6, for 15–20 minutes. Turn out on to racks to cool.

Serve hot, warm or cold with brandy butter, cream or cream with some Cider Brandy or the like whisked into it.

I don't know how I have held off for so long, how this recipe hasn't nudged its way to the top of the chapter, since my relationship with chocolate is as deep and intense as the stuff itself. Yes, this chocolate pie is rich, heavy, cold, dark, wicked, girth – rather than death – defying, and utterly, utterly seductive. What more could you want from a pudding, nay, from life itself!

Chocolate Pie with Mocha Cream

SERVES 8

Cookie-crumb base:

225g/8oz chocolate cookies, plain, not covered in chocolate. I use Baker and Spice's, but most supermarkets make their own

1 tbsp Green and Black's organic cocoa powder

110g/4oz unsalted butter, melted

Filling:

2 eggs

3 egg yolks

40g/1½oz caster sugar

140g/5oz unsalted butter

200g/7oz best bitter chocolate with 70% cocoa solids, Valrhona, Green and Black or The Chocolate Society, broken into pieces

Topping:

290ml/10fl oz double cream, Jersey if possible

2 tsp instant espresso coffee dissolved in 2 tbsp of the cream

1–2 tbsp unrefined icing sugar

Put the cookies and cocoa powder in a food processor and blitz to crumbs. Add the melted butter and process again to combine. Take a 23cm/9in tart tin, deep rather than shallow and with a removable base, line with the mixture and refrigerate.

To make the filling, put the eggs, yolks and caster sugar into a bowl and beat together vigorously, preferably with an electric whisk, until really thick and fluffy. Melt the butter and chocolate together in a bowl over a saucepan of barely simmering water – don't let the bottom of the bowl touch it – and stir until smooth. Pour on to the egg mixture while still warm, and beat together briefly until well amalgamated. Pour into the cold, crumb crust and refrigerate for a few hours.

Whisk the cream up to an hour before you want to eat the pudding, then add the dissolved espresso and cream. Sift over the first tablespoon of icing sugar and continue to beat until it holds softly. Spoon over the pie and refrigerate for an hour before serving. You can grate a little chocolate finely over the top and add the other spoonful of icing sugar if you feel like it.

Soured cream works well with acidic fruit like cherries and apples. You can use three beaten eggs with the soured cream and turn the filling into a custard, or do what I prefer, coat the fruit stickily with the double hit of sharp/sweet, sour cream and sugar.

Sour Cream Cherry Pie

SERVES 6

675g/1½lb cherries, stoned
  with a cherry stoner, or use
  the Morello cherries that you
  can buy in a jar
142ml/5fl oz carton soured
  cream
110g/4oz light muscovado
  sugar, or to taste
1 egg white
demerara sugar for the top,
  optional
shortcrust pastry made with
  340g/12oz flour and 170/6oz
  unsalted butter (see p.140)

Combine all the filling ingredients in a large bowl and leave for 15 minutes or so. Roll out the pastry into two large circles, one a little larger than the other.

Preheat the oven to 200°C/400°F/Gas 6. Line a greased pie dish with the larger circle of pastry, then mix the fruits, sugar and cream again and tip them into the pie dish, mounding them up in the centre. Place the second piece of pastry over the top and crimp the edges together. Cut a hole for the steam to escape through and decorate with a pastry bunch of cherries if you have any leftovers. Brush the top with egg white and throw over a little demerara sugar.

Bake for 20 minutes, then reduce the temperature to 180°C/350°F/Gas 4 and continue to cook for 30 minutes or until browned and bubbling. Serve warm or cold with more cream.

This is a lovely pie from Elisabeth Lambert Ortiz's book *Best of Caribbean Cooking*. Lime magically makes mangoes taste more mango-like. It has the same effect when spritzed on melon.

Mango Pie

SERVES 6
1 large ripe mango weighing
   about 750g/1lb 10oz, or two
   which weigh rather more, a
   good kilo/2¼lb
3 tbsp fresh lime juice
110g/4oz unrefined sugar
1 level tbsp arrowroot mixed
   with 3 tbsp water

Pastry:
170g/6oz plain flour
1 tbsp sugar
a pinch of salt
85g/3oz unsalted butter
30g/1oz lard, chilled and cut
   into small pieces

Sift the dry ingredients for the pastry together into a large bowl, then rub in the fats until the mixture is crumbly. Add 3 tablespoons of ice-cold water and mix together to a stiffish dough. Chill for at least 30 minutes.

Preheat the oven to 180°C/350°F/Gas 4. Roll out the pastry and line a 23cm/9in greased pie plate. Bake blind for 25 minutes or until golden brown (see p. 140). Remove the greaseproof and beans for the last 5 minutes to let the pastry dry out. Leave to cool.

To make the filling, peel the mango over a plate so that no juice is wasted. Cut two good wide slices down each side, to the central seed, and put them on a plate. Cut the slices into long strips and sprinkle them with some lime juice. Remove the rest of the pulp from the seed and measure it. There should be about 240ml/8fl oz. Put the pulp into a pan with the rest of the lime juice, sugar and 3 tablespoons of water. Simmer until soft, about 10 minutes, then liquidize and return to the pan. Stir up the arrowroot and add to the mango pulp. Cook until thickened, stirring all the time. Cool slightly. If the consistency is too gluey, dilute with extra water.

Arrange the mango slices in the cold pastry case in an overlapping pattern. Use the shorter pieces to fill in the sides. Spoon the purée over the strips to make an even coating and chill thoroughly. Serve plain or with custard, whipped cream or vanilla ice cream

These are really pears stuffed with a boozy frangipane-spiced cream and wrapped in puff pastry. I leave the pear stalks on so they poke out of the bronzed leaves of buttery pastry. Easier than they sound and both beautiful and delicious.

The Italian Pear Pie is a simple dish made festive and slightly medieval with crushed amaretti and a rose-flower water icing.

Pear Pies

SERVES 6

6 ripe but firm pears
285g/10oz unrefined caster
    sugar
6 cloves
zest of 2 lemons
2 tbsp lemon juice
a stick of cinnamon
4 tbsp freshly ground almonds
a few drops of bitter almond
    extract (from Culpeper's)
2 tbsp brandy
1 tbsp soft butter
225g/8oz puff pastry (see p.141)
beaten egg for glaze

Core the pears from their bases, leaving the stalks on. Put the caster sugar, cloves, zest, juice and cinnamon in a pan with 750ml/1 pint 7fl oz water and stir together. Add the pears, bring to the boil and simmer gently for 6 minutes. Remove the pears and dry them. Reduce the syrup by letting it bubble away for 5 or 6 minutes. In a bowl, mix the ground almonds with the almond extract, brandy and butter. Stuff the cored bases of the pears with this mixture.

Preheat the oven to 200°C/400°F/Gas 6. Roll out the pastry and divide into 6 pieces. Wrap each pear in a piece of pastry, brush with beaten egg and stand them on a baking sheet. Bake for 30 minutes or until the pastry has puffed up and turned golden. Serve with the sugar syrup and splodges of crème fraîche on the side.

Italian Pear Pie

SERVES 6

8 pears, peeled, cored and
    sliced
lemon juice
light muscovado sugar
6 large or 12 small amaretti
a knife point of cinnamon
shortcrust pastry made with
    340g/12oz flour and 170g/6oz
    unsalted butter (see p.140)

Icing:
2 tbsp unrefined caster sugar
55g/2oz unsalted butter
3 tbsp rose-flower water
110g/4oz unrefined icing sugar

Preheat the oven to 200°C/400°F/Gas 6. Grease a deep, 23cm/9in pie tin and line it with a little over half the pastry. Toss the pear slices in a little lemon juice and light muscovado sugar – be sparing with the sugar. Add the crushed amaretti and cinnamon, then put everything into the pastry case. Cover with the rest of the pastry and make a hole for the steam to escape. Bake for 15 minutes, then turn the heat down to 180°C/350°F/Gas 4 and bake until the pie and the fruit are cooked through, about another 30 minutes.

Put the caster sugar, butter and rose-flower water into a pan and bring to boiling point. Tip the mixture on to the sifted icing sugar in a bowl and beat until satiny smooth. Spread over the warm pie with a palette knife and serve tepid. You can slake whipped cream with a little eau de vie de poire to serve with it if you feel suitably epicurean.

Curiously, the intensity of the blackcurrants does not vanquish the flavour of the pears in this recipe. Instead it enhances them. You can prepare the sweet pastry (pâte sucrée) and the fruit filling in advance, leaving the last-minute whisking of the meringue until just before you want to put the pie in the oven.

Pear and Blackcurrant Meringue Pie

SERVES 6–8
1kg/2¼lb pears
140g/5oz blackcurrants or redcurrants
140g/5oz unrefined sugar
3 egg whites
100g/3½oz unrefined caster sugar

Pâte sucrée:
110g/4oz soft butter
2 tbsp vanilla caster sugar
1 large egg
pinch salt
225g/8oz plain flour

To make the pastry, cream the butter and sugar in a food processor, then add the egg and salt. When the mixture is reasonably well amalgamated, add the flour. The dough should need no water. Chill in the fridge for at least 30 minutes, an hour is better. Bake blind in the usual way (see p.140), but do not allow the pastry to brown at this stage; aim for pale gold.

Peel, core and slice the pears. Put the currants into a pan with the sugar and bring them to simmering point. After a couple of minutes plop in the pears and let them cook very gently for about 15 minutes. Turn them so that they absorb the currant colour evenly, but do not let them cook so long that they lose their shape completely.

Preheat the oven to 180°C/350°F/Gas 4. Spread the fruit over the cooled pastry base. Whisk the egg whites stiffly, then add half the sugar and whisk again for your life, before folding in the rest of the sugar. Add the meringue to the pie, spreading it right to the edges. Bake for about 20 minutes or until the meringue has browned and crisped. Eat warm with cream.

This is a pudding that strays across the line of kitsch. It is a tad brash and overt in its vulgarity, but so disarmingly delicious that it manages to qualify on the other kind of good taste grounds alone. Besides, cutting deep chasms of crimson raspberry into the ice cream and making the Jackson Pollock swirly patterned top is such fun, as is pouring the final libation of raspberry sauce into a deep, sharp, sugary puddle around each slice.

Finally, it is easy. You can make it one step at a time, in individual tart tins or in one large ring, starting the day before you need it, and you don't even need to open the oven door.

Raspberry Ripple Ice Cream Pie

SERVES 6–8

Cookie-crumb base:
225g/8oz chocolate cookies, plain not covered in chocolate, I use Baker and Spice's, but most supermarkets make their own
1 tbsp Green and Black's organic cocoa powder
110g/4oz unsalted butter, melted

Filling:
1 vanilla pod
570ml/1 pint Jersey milk
6 egg yolks
110g/4oz unrefined caster sugar
2 tsp cornflour
290ml/10fl oz double cream

Raspberry sauce:
225g/8oz fresh or frozen raspberries (you can double these quantities and the sugar below if you like lashings of sauce)
55g/2oz unrefined caster sugar
a little lemon juice

To make the cookie crust, put the cookies and cocoa powder in a food processor and blitz to crumbs. Add the melted butter and process again to combine. Take a 23cm/9in tart tin, deep rather than shallow and with a removable base, line with cookie-crust mixture and refrigerate.

Remove the seeds from the split vanilla pod and place them with the pod and the milk in a saucepan. Bring to the boil, remove from the heat, cover and leave the milk to infuse for 30 minutes. Take the pod out and wash and dry it to store in your vanilla caster sugar jar.

In a separate bowl, beat together the egg yolks, sugar and cornflour. Pour the milk over them, whisking as you go, and return the whole lot to the pan. Cook over a low heat for up to 10 minutes, whisking, until the mixture thickens. Pour into a bowl and set aside to cool quickly over a bowl of ice or by putting it in the freezer. Whisk the cream and fold it into the cold custard, then transfer the mixture to the freezer for 30 minutes until it begins to thicken.

To make the raspberry sauce, blitz the raspberries in a food processor, sieve them into a bowl and add sugar to taste. Stir until the sugar has dissolved. Add a squeeze of lemon to bring out the flavour.

Scrape the ice cream into the cookie crust, then, with a dessertspoon, cut down into the ice cream with spoons of the raspberry sauce so that it penetrates as far down as possible. Keep the rest of the sauce to pour over later. Freeze overnight or, if you've made it in the morning, until you want it for dinner. Transfer to the fridge for 30 minutes before you want to eat it, then ease the tin away and serve with a jug of raspberry sauce.

The Nellie Melba of pies this, with the custard, homemade and scented with grains of vanilla, funnelled down through the pie crust for the last 10 minutes of cooking. The Americans still call two-fruit pies 'marriage pies' and this is a perfect union. A real high-summer pie, its colours beauteous to behold.

Peach and Raspberry Custard Pie

SERVES 6

6 ripe peaches, skinned, halved, stoned, then each half cut into four

2 punnets or about 340g/12oz raspberries

55g/2oz or to taste unrefined caster sugar

2 dsrtsp cornflour

shortcrust pastry made with 225g/8oz flour and 110g/4oz unsalted butter (see p.140)

Custard:

vanilla pod

570ml/1 pint Jersey milk

6 egg yolks

85g/3oz unrefined caster sugar

Preheat the oven to 230°C/450°F/Gas 8. Put the fruit, sugar and cornflour into a large bowl. Give everything a gentle turn and leave to macerate for at least 15 minutes. Pile the mixture into your pie dish, mounding it up in the middle. Cover with the pastry crust in the usual way, either making a steam hole or cutting a shape or series of shapes into the top crust before you cover the pie. Bake for 15 minutes before turning the oven down to 180°C/360°F/Gas 4 for the next 25 minutes.

The pie is great just like this if you don't feel like doing anything else. Otherwise, make the custard. Scrape the seeds out of a vanilla pod and put them into a pan with the pod and a pint of Jersey milk. Bring to the boil, cover and remove from the heat, and leave for 15 minutes to infuse. Whisk together the egg yolks and caster sugar, then strain the infused milk over them. Whisk some more and return the mixture to the pan. Cook, while stirring or whisking, over a gentle heat until the custard thickens. Ten minutes should do it.

Remove the pie from the oven and funnel as much custard as you can down the central steam hole. If you have cut a larger shape in the pastry crust it will pour all the more readily. Return to the oven for a final 10 minutes. Prepare to be stunned.

Just a glorious pie. Blackcurrants have an extraordinary intensity of flavour when they are cooked and also an extraordinary intensity of flavour when they are raw. Both are completely different and that says a lot for the alchemy of cooking – for the way it transforms tastes and textures, colours and scents.

Blackcurrant Pie

SERVES 6–8

675g/1½lb blackcurrants stripped from their stems with the tines of a fork

110g/4oz unrefined granulated sugar, or to taste

1 tbsp cornflour

demerara sugar for sprinkling

shortcrust pastry made with 340g/12oz flour and 170g/6oz unsalted butter (see p.140)

a beaten egg

Throw the fruit into a bowl, toss it with the sugar and leave to macerate for about 30 minutes. Pour off the accumulated juice into a small bowl, sift in the cornflour and stir together until smooth.

Preheat the oven to 200°C/400°F/Gas 6. Line a greased deep pie dish with just over half the pastry, add the fruits, then tip over the juice. Roll out the topcoat of pastry, and lay it over the fruit, sealing the edges with the tines of a fork. Cut holes for the steam to escape through and brush with a beaten egg.

Bake for 20 minutes, then turn the heat down to 180°C/350°F/Gas 4 and continue to cook for a further 30 minutes or until golden brown. Brush with a little more beaten egg and sprinkle with a handful of demerara sugar at half time if you want a crunchy sugared top. Serve hot with plenty of thin pouring cream.

The golden rule for pastry is cold, cold, cold. Your butter should be chilled, your hands cold and you need a cold slab to roll the pastry out on. If you use a food processor, stop the button the minute the flour and butter have cohered into a ball. Warmth and overworking are the enemies of good pastry.

PIE PASTRY

Shortcrust pastry

Use twice the weight of plain flour (preferably organic) to unsalted butter – see individual recipes for quantities. Some recipes call for half butter, half lard.

Sift the flour and a pinch of sea salt into a food processor, then cut the cold butter into small pieces on top of it. I process it for 20–30 seconds, then add ice-cold water through the top, a tablespoon at a time – 2–2½ should do it – with the machine running. If the paste is still in crumbly little bits after a minute or two, add a tablespoon more water, but remember, the more water you use, the more the pastry will shrink if you bake it blind. One solution is to use a bit of cream or egg yolk instead of water. The moment the dough has cohered into a single ball, stop, remove it, wrap it in clingfilm and put it in the fridge for at least 30 minutes.

If you're making pastry by hand, sift the flour into a large bowl with the salt, add the chopped butter and work as briskly as you can to rub the fat into the flour. Use the tips of your fingers only, rather like running grains of hot sand through your fingers. Add the water bit by bit as above; wrap and chill the pastry.

If you're making a double-crust pie, divide the pastry into roughly two-thirds and one-third. Then scatter a bit of flour on your work surface, roll your rolling pin in it, dust the palms of your hands, and start rolling. Always roll away from yourself, tuning the pastry as you go, and keep the rolling pin and work surface floured to prevent sticking.

Baking blind

If you're baking your pastry case blind, preheat the oven to 190–200°C/375–400°F/Gas 5–6. Line your greased pie tin with pastry. Never stretch it, it will stretch back. Try to leave at least 30 minutes for the unbaked pastry to commune with the inside of your fridge. Or put it in the night before you need it.

Tear off a piece of greaseproof paper a little larger than the tart tin and place it over the pastry. Cover the paper with a layer of dried beans; the idea is to prevent the pastry from rising up in the oven. When the pastry is nearly cooked (the timing depends on the rest of the recipe), remove the paper and beans and prick the base of the pastry to let out trapped air that would otherwise bubble up. Return the tart to the oven for 5–10 minutes to dry the pastry base. Brushing the partly baked pastry case with a light coating of beaten egg or egg white ensures a crisp finished tart.

Puff pastry

170g/6oz plain flour
a pinch of salt
170g/6oz unsalted butter
about 150ml/5fl oz cold water

Sift the flour and salt into a mixing bowl, then rub in 25g/1oz of the butter, as for shortcrust pastry, or use a food processor. Mix in the water and then gently knead the dough on a floured surface, preferably marble. Wrap it in clingfilm and refrigerate for 30 minutes.

Keep the rest of the butter out so that it softens, then flatten it into a rectangle 2.5cm/1in thick. On a lightly floured surface, roll out the dough into a rectangle three times the length and 2.5cm/1in wider than the rectangle of butter. Place the butter in the centre of the pastry and then fold over the top and bottom of the pastry to cover the butter.

With the rolling pin, press down on the edges to seal in the butter, then give the dough a quarter turn clockwise. Now roll the dough out so that it returns to its original length. Fold over the ends again, press them together with the rolling pin, and give a further quarter-turn clockwise. Repeat the process once more, then rest the dough in the fridge for at least 30 minutes, remembering which way it is facing.

Repeat the rolling and turning process twice more, then refrigerate for a final 30 minutes before using or freezing. If the pastry gets warm and buttery at any stage during the process, put it in the fridge to chill.

If you prefer not to make your own, you can buy a 1kg/2¼lb sheet of wonderful ready-made puff pastry from Baker & Spice, 46 Walton Street, London SW3 1RB. Tel: 0207 589 4734. It's made with best French flour and butter and worth every penny.

Index

First published in the United Kingdom in 2003 by
Weidenfeld & Nicolson
an imprint of the Orion Publishing Group
Wellington House
125 Strand
London WC2 0BB

This edition first published in the United Kingdom in 2004 by
Weidenfeld & Nicolson

A CIP catalogue record for this book is available from the British Library

ISBN 0 297 84376 1

Printed and bound in Italy

Design director David Rowley
Editorial director Susan Haynes
Designed by Nigel Soper
Edited by Jinny Johnson
Proofread by Gwen Rigby
Index by Elizabeth Wiggans